The Arts & Crafts

COLLECTOR'S GUIDE

The Arts & Crafts

COLLECTOR'S GUIDE

David Rago

with Suzanne Sliker

& David Rudd

PHOTOGRAPHS BY
David Rago

Gibbs Smith, Publisher
Salt Lake City

First Edition
09 08 07 06 05   5 4 3 2 1

PUBLISHED BY
Gibbs Smith, Publisher
P.O. Box 667
Layton, Utah 84041

Orders: 1.800.748.5439
www.gibbs-smith.com

Designed by Steve Rachwal
Printed and bound in Hong Kong

Library of Congress Cataloging-in-Publication Data
Rago, David.
   The arts & crafts collector's guide / by David Rago with
Suzanne Sliker and David Rudd.— 1st ed.
      p. cm.
   ISBN 1-58685-052-0
   1. Arts and crafts movement—United States—Collectors
and collecting. 2. Art pottery—United States—Collectors and
collecting. I. Title: Arts and crafts collector's guide. II.
Sliker, Suzanne. III. Rudd, David, 1954- IV. Title.
NK1141.R28 2005
738'.075—dc22
                              2004024263

Front cover images
   Top left: Newcomb College pot
   Bottom left: Dirk Van Erp lamp
   Right: Charles Rohlfs chair

Back cover images
   Top left: L. and J. G. Stickley clock
   Bottom left: English Arts and Crafts lantern
   Bottom right: Brouwer pot

I would like to thank my parents Domenic and Mary Rago for sparking my interest in art pottery, Elaine Small Piechota for her early support, and Suzanne Perrault, my wife.

Contents

Introduction

AFTER CONSIDERING ALL OF THE BOOKS currently available on American Arts and Crafts, I came to the conclusion that there was a need for an insider's guide on collecting Arts and Crafts material. Or, more to the point, there's a dearth of books that discuss what's good, what's still reasonably priced, and what's likely to either bring you a great deal of enjoyment, increase in value, or both.

I'm not interested in rehashing the history of the Arts and Crafts period, or even detailing facts about individual makers and their work. Better, more patient authors established that foundation long ago and still more are in the process of adding to that body of work.

Rather, my thirty plus years of experience have focused on eschewing scholarly works on the subject. It's not that I'm an anti-intellectual snob. I've just always learned better by handling something than by simply reading about it. I'd much rather, for example, touch a piece of Grueby pottery than have someone tell me how it feels.

That, of course, leaves you having to read about Grueby pottery instead of actually wrapping your fingers around a piece. Nevertheless, I can offer insight into collecting period pieces, tell you where you're most likely to get the opportunity to see such things for yourself, and prepare you well for the experience.

This book is infected with my personal biases about what's worth buying. The one thing I have in any quantity is opinions about American Arts and Crafts. I encourage you, however, to be dismissive of any advice contained in this book that doesn't speak directly to your own experience, especially if you've done the work necessary to develop your own opinions.

This guide covers the four main areas of Arts and Crafts material: art pottery, mission furniture, wrought metal, and period lighting. These chapters are well illustrated with photos from David Rago Auctions' voluminous archive (mostly from the Craftsman Auction series), including detailed photos showing what I mean by terms such as *through tenons, hand thrown,* and *patina.*

I dread the thought of another suggested reading list, so, instead, I've included a Further Reading section at the end of this book that discusses the noteworthy contributions of authors whose writings should be in any serious Arts and Crafts library.

I encourage you to explore the wealth of information available at your fingertips at our specialized Web site, www.ragoarts.com. It's free, updated regularly, and provides answers to many questions that inevitably arise from time to time.

Another fantastic resource is our magazine, *Style: 1900.* We began publication over fifteen years ago as of this writing. The magazine is filled with information about the dealers and auction houses that specialize in this period, annual conferences, museum shows, and new research. It is $25 per year well spent.

I would like to conclude this introduction by giving you some of the best advice I've received over the years on buying pieces. While I might accurately be accused of not having much in the way of original thought, I have been blessed with the capacity to recognize valuable information when it passes in front of me.

- THERE'S NEVER A RUSH TO BUY A PIECE. Something similar or in better condition will almost always come along later. Most bad purchases are those made in haste.

- BUY WITH YOUR HEART, BUT KEEP AN EYE COCKED TO THE FUTURE. To be clear, you have to buy the things that bring you joy, but if you overspend, you'll enjoy them less.

- A HAIRLINE IS ALWAYS SHORTER IF YOU'RE TRYING TO SELL A PIECE.

CRAFTSPEOPLE FROM THE ARTS AND CRAFTS PERIOD MADE A CONSCIOUS EFFORT TO MAKE SOULFUL OBJECTS. Each object embodies the soul of the artist who crafted it. You must shut down your mind and let the object register on a deeper level. Elbert Hubbard may have been a salesman, and maybe even a charlatan, as some have claimed, but the Roycroft pieces are almost spooky in the amount of spirit they contain.

TO QUOTE WILLIAM J. WALLEY, "There is more merit in a brick modeled and finished by hand than in the best piece of molded pottery ever made."

TRUST YOUR INSTINCTS. It's easy to become lost in the words of experts who adeptly present a great deal of highly detailed information. Many, however, lack understanding of the object and its heart. I have seen the deepest of understanding in the most inarticulate of people.

YOU CAN LEARN SOMETHING ABOUT ARTS AND CRAFTS FROM ANYONE, even if it's only to better understand what you don't like. I've been constantly humbled by the insights of the uninformed and annoyed by the rantings of the educated.

ART IS LIKE FRIENDS: if you don't overlook a few faults, you won't have any.

History of Collecting
in the Arts and Crafts Market

IN SOME RESPECTS, THERE'S ALWAYS BEEN A SECOND-
ARY MARKET FOR ARTS AND CRAFTS MATERIAL. People's
interest in Rookwood pottery has never waned. They've been
displaying it in cupboards and on mantel tops as decorative art
since its beginnings. I make this point because this chapter not so
much discusses the entire history of Arts and Crafts, but rather
the revival of interest in the Arts and Crafts period, beginning
around 1970.

During the late 1960s, a number of books were published on
various potteries, including Rookwood, Roseville, and Weller.
Herbert Peck's first book on the Rookwood Pottery heralded a
string of tomes on Arts and
Crafts that has increased
exponentially with each
passing year.

ROOKWOOD VASE
Maker: *William P. McDonald*
Date Made: *1899*
Dimensions: *11¼" x 6¼"*
Value: *$60,000–80,000*

*Sea green Rookwood vase, with a
panoramic view in relief of a large
seagull against crashing waves
at dawn. Painted in tones of blue,
pink, green, and black.*

It was not until 1974, however, with the opening of the
Princeton University exhibition
Arts and Crafts in America and
the publication of the accom-
panying scholarly catalog, that
a relatively disparate group of
collectors realized they repre-
sented a viable force. Spread
across America, comprised of
college professors, teachers,
flea marketers, homemakers,
and the occasional college
student, they were united in
their attraction to this unher-
alded art ware.

ROOKWOOD VASE

Maker: *Kataro Shirayamadani*
Date Made: *1899*
Dimensions: *12½" x 5"*
Value: *$35,000–40,000*

Tall Rookwood vase painted with a heron spreading its wings amidst a bronze lotus blossom and lily pads. Bottom wrapped in a bronze overlay of flowers and large leaves.

The 1970s

THE DECADE OF THE 1970S WAS A DEFINING TIME FOR THIS PERIOD. It's easy to wax nostalgic about those days, and hard not to laugh at the bad choices that nearly everyone involved made. For example, during one of my own bouts of youthful ignorance nearly thirty years ago, I made a hurried and uninformed sale of a most important example of Van Briggle pottery.

The piece, I was to later learn, had been made for the 1904 St. Louis World's Fair, the awareness of which would have explained the 1903 date. The pot itself was a fairly bland, tapering cylinder with two short strap handles near the top. It was covered with an unexceptional raspberry matte glaze. This dull foundation was merely a foil, however, for two exquisitely detailed bronze dragonflies, their bodies running down the handles and

their wings wrapping around the top, meeting halfway around the opening. Their eyes were opal cabochons.

I had found the pot one Sunday morning at a local flea market, Marge's Pottery Barn in Lambertville, New Jersey. I spent about $500, a princely sum for the time. I should point out that this was about three weeks' net pay at the supermarket where I was working night crew. Unfortunately, I knew enough to know to buy the pot and not enough to know how to sell it. In a confluence of fear, ignorance, and haste, I rushed a sale that netted a profit of a few dollars. On today's market, the vase (no longer a pot at these levels) would be worth $50,000 to $75,000.

That particular learning experience was the flip side of thousands of really good ones. It was a very exciting time to be involved in Arts and Crafts because blissful ignorance clearly cut both ways, with unexpected finds and foolish choices.

Some very cool things turned up at flea markets and yard sales back in the 1970s, and when they did the prices were usually measured in the tens of dollars. But it is equally true that only a fraction of what existed began to surface because that same lack of awareness contributed to sellers' general lack of understanding. If you didn't think it was worth anything, why devote valuable table space at an antiques show or flea market? Additionally, you could certainly have purchased a great piece of high-glazed Newcomb pottery for under $100, but it wasn't worth more than double that at the time, and there were precious few people

NEWCOMB COLLEGE VASE
Maker: *Sadie Irvine*
Date Made: *ca 1915*
Dimensions: *10" x 6¼"*
Value: *$17,500—22,500*

Large Newcomb College vase carved with a nighttime landscape, with palm trees in tones of blue and green and a bright yellow moon. Production number JM/W72/150.

GUSTAV STICKLEY DESK/BOOKCASE

Maker: Harvey Ellis
Date Made: *1903*
Dimensions: *56" x 56" x 15"*
Value: *$100,000–125,000*

A Gustav Stickley fine desk/bookcase with a drop-front desk over two drawers and flanked by two bookcase doors with leaded-glass panels and iron hardware. Original finish with original interior, including inkwells. Minor chip on the top and a few repaired chips. Probably purchased from Gustav Stickley, the desk descended through the family of a chief judge of the U.S. District Court in New Jersey.

David Rago at Brimfield, 1978.

around to buy it. (And prime examples of Stickley furniture, favored by only a few, often doubled as workbenches or porch furniture.)

In 1977, on my seventh trip to the fabled Brimfield Flea Market in Massachusetts, I covered the field tirelessly. While I might have missed a pot or two, I brought home 172 pieces of pottery after three days of picking. I am not exaggerating when I say I filled my blue Chevy cargo van to the rooftop with boxes of ceramics. My scores ranged from a $5 production planter to a Weller masterpiece that ended up in the Boston Museum of Fine Arts show called The Art That Is Life a decade later.

On the other hand, if I totaled the expected profits from those purchases, my net gain would have likely been less than $4,000. So much those days was buying a piece for $30 and selling it for $50, or paying $250 for a $300 pot. There were no specialty Arts and Crafts auctions at the time and only one gallery in the nation devoted to the Arts and Crafts. Further, though publications on the subject were slowly finding their way to the shelves of bookstores and libraries, they examined the history of these pieces instead of defining the future for collecting them.

A case in point was the persistent emphasis on mission furniture by Gustav Stickley and art pottery designed in the Victorian

GUSTAV STICKLEY PIANO-ROLL CABINET

Date Made: *ca 1910*
Dimensions: *51" x 33" x 18"*
Value: *$7,500–10,000*

Gustav Stickley rare piano-roll cabinet with two paneled doors and iron V-pulls. Original finish, with some finish loss to front. Custom made for an Adirondack camp by Gustav Stickley and may be unique. Red decal inside upper left and a paper label on the back.

style. The former proved to be only partially correct, and the latter almost entirely wrong. To collect Arts and Crafts in the 1970s was to inhabit the land of the blind. Those of us living at that time were all too willing to follow the few with one eye.

Beyond the Princeton University show of 1974, perhaps the single most important thing to happen to the field was the opening of the Jordan-Volpe Gallery in 1975. While much newspaper ink has described some curious business practices by the Volpe end of that partnership, no one can dispute the impact that single New York City gallery had on the field. It is safe to say that, to this day, much of the interest in Arts and Crafts, people's appreciation of what's "great" and their willingness to pay high prices, can be traced back to that handsome, street-level loft space on West Broadway.

It was part of the gallery's snob appeal that led to the feverish collecting of Gustav Stickley furniture, to the exclusion of nearly everything else. Certainly, the random piece by Charles Rohlfs or Frank Lloyd Wright could be found sparingly situated on the gallery's carpeted floor under the crisp glint of theater lighting, but there wasn't much.

Todd Volpe himself, under whom I was later to work for nearly three years, told me during an offhanded sales pitch that, while he had some lesser things to sell me, I "deserved" to buy only Gustav Stickley. I came to understand this bias was a product of

ROOKWOOD VASE
Date Made: *1882*
Dimensions: *11 ½" x 6 ½"*
Value: *$3,000–4,000*

Early Japanese hand-thrown flaring Rookwood vase, carved with abstract square pattern, medallion, and script, and the stooped figure of an Oriental peasant in high relief in green, brown, and blue against a tan ground. Red crayon numbers on bottom. Deaccessioned from the Cincinnati Museum and catalogued in Stanley Burt's inventory.

those times, a time when making a case for collecting Arts and Crafts demanded the focus to be placed on what was perceived to be the very best. The incomplete scholarship of the day led to the misconception that this "very best" was exclusively Gustav Stickley, to the detriment of works by the legion of companies sharing, in some capacity, his surname.

The same incomplete awareness that led to the deification of Gustav Stickley similarly contributed to the pursuit of Victorian-inspired decorative ceramics. The purists reading this will argue correctly that some of the greatest collections of Grueby and Ohr pottery came out of this period. In response, I contend that those very collectors have probably spent a great deal of time and money buying hand-painted aberrations such as early Rookwood, Limoges-type Wheatley, and some beautiful, if ill-fated, portraitures.

As one of my early mentors Rosalie Berberian lucidly explained, the Ohio Valley School of ceramic design focused on painting

ROOKWOOD VASE

Maker: *Kataro Shirayamadani*
Date Made: *1887*
Dimensions: *18" x 6"*
Value: *$5,000–7,500*

Tall Rookwood vase delicately painted in fine detail with wild roses in heavy slip relief in tones of dark green and brown on a diagonally shaded brown-and-green ground. Unglazed.

decoration onto the surface of the pot. The clay vessel served as a canvas, and the quality of each example depended on how well the flower, or land-scape, or native brave was painted, and how perfectly the heat of the kiln finished the job. What she was also describing was the separation of design and medium, one of the tacit definitions of Victorian-inspired ware.

ROOKWOOD VASE
Maker: *Matthew A. Daly*
Date Made: *1900*
Dimensions: *16" x 15"*
Value: *$70,000–80,000*

American Indian portrait pillow vase. Arguably the best example of its kind. Striking detail of a Native American chief in full headdress and breastplate. Signed on the front with chief's name: "Chief Hollow Horn Bear, Sioux, MA." Standard glaze.

Those of us buying and selling art pottery back in that day thought this hand-painted ware to be the pinnacle of achievement. It was one of the few things that was easy to understand and evaluate. Was the Falstaff portrait sharp or, during firing, did the slip painting that was once his left eye run down to the vicinity of his chin? Even two perfectly fired examples, when compared side by side, could show to a young and untrained eye that Arthur Williams was nearly always a far better painter than Arthur Dunleavy.

Complicating matters further was the verity that, piece for piece, the work produced by Ohio Valley companies like Rookwood had long been regarded as the premier pottery in America. If you could go back in time a mere forty years and peek into the best collections of art pottery, such as those gathered by David Glover or Elliot and Enid Wysor, you would see a spellbinding array of some of the best Victorian ware ever assembled, and a relative smattering of other things.

Early collectors proved their keen discernment by adding to their holdings pieces of Art Nouveau and Moderne ware of similar quality and importance. But, buying as they did in the 1960s and early 1970s, they bought what they understood to be the best in quality (correctly) and the best in design (less so). (As I write this, we just received for auction sixty pieces of Rookwood pottery collected by a true, yet obscure, pioneer during the 1950s and 1960s. Only six of these pieces date 1897 or later; the rest are fine but derivative examples of early lines such as standard glaze, cameo, Limoges-type, and bisque.)

ROOKWOOD PITCHER
Maker: *Albert R. Valentien*
Date Made: *1884*
Dimensions: *8¼" x 6¼"*
Value: *$2,000–2,500*

Early Rookwood pitcher painted in the Japanese style, with brown crabs on a speckled sea green ground.

OHR VASE

Maker: *George Ohr*
Date Made: *1900*
Dimensions: *6¾" x 4½"*
Value: *$20,000–25,000*

Large flaring Ohr vase with ruffled stovepipe base and dimpled top with torn, floriform rim covered in mottled indigo glaze. Several nicks to rim. Stamped "G.E. Ohr, Biloxi, Miss."

The aforementioned Ms. Berberian, in one of her many moments of prescience, told me in the late 1970s that this preoccupation with hand-painted ware would come to an abrupt halt at some point. Indeed, as handsome and intriguing as the best Rookwood pottery was, there was a growing awareness of pottery made by Arts and Crafts masters such as Boston's William Grueby, the young ladies of New Orleans' Newcomb College, and the wacky manipulations of Biloxi, Mississippi,

NEWCOMB COLLEGE VASE
Maker: *Sabina Wells*
Date Made: *ca 1905*
Dimensions: *9½" x 6½"*
Value: *$9,000–12,000*

Early, large, pear-shaped Newcomb College vase carved with large blue blossoms and green leaves on an ivory-and-light-blue ground. Opposing lines to rim. Production number NC/SEWELLS/ss38/W.

master George Ohr. Ms. Berberian might have been surprised only at how quickly that interest flourished.

The foundation of interest in Arts and Crafts was established during the 1970s. While there was a great deal of confusion about what the Arts and Crafts was, it was a time when a large number of people began to understand the validity of the period. Nevertheless, as unexpected as these first ten years were, things would soon get much more interesting.

The 1980s

The second decade of Arts and Crafts collecting got off to a rocky start because of the recession of the Carter presidency. While prices were still modest in comparison to contemporary levels, they were at an all-time high when the '80s began. These new price levels brought other, "lesser," goods to the forefront of the market.

GUSTAV STICKLEY DIRECTOR'S TABLE

Date Made: *ca 1905*
Dimensions: *30" x 72" x 36 ½"*
Value: *$30,000–35,000*

Gustav Stickley rare director's table with overhanging rectangular top, broad apron, and shoe feet. Good original finish and color (rarely found with original finish to top). Screw holes under top. Red decal inside shoe foot.

CHARLES ROHLFS TALL-BACK HALL CHAIR

Date Made: *1900*
Dimensions: *57" x 18" x 15"*
Value: *$30,000–35,000*

Tall-back hall chair with reticulated spine. Carved and cutout details, faceted pegs, and a semicircular seat. Old, very light overcoat and chip to finial. Branded CR/1900.

One reason many pioneering collectors turned to Arts and Crafts material in the first place was because they had little money to furnish and decorate their homes. Arts and Crafts pieces were quite inexpensive through the early 1970s. A decade later, it is worth noting that, because of the redefined pricing structure of the more established brands such as Gustav Stickley and Charles Rohlfs, more conservative collectors began to pursue other period makers.

While the emphasis on mission oak furniture was still on strong forms in mint condition, there was a decided shift away from just Gustav to works by his better-regarded contemporaries such as L. and J. G. Stickley and the Limbert Furniture Company. One pleasant surprise during this time was that not only could such pieces be as good as most of Gustav's work, but in some cases they were better.

LIMBERT PLANT STAND

Date Made: *ca 1905*
Dimensions: *28 ¼" x 18" x 18"*
Value: *$2,000–2,500*

Rare Limbert plant stand with octagonal overhanging top, corbels, and two square cutouts to each side. Overcoat to original finish on base and refinished top. Paper label.

Limbert pieces, for example, run the gamut from European elegance to spindly cheapness. It's easy to dismiss Limbert work if you study only their thin approximations of standard mission forms. The quality of construction, wood selection, and overall line is purely derivative. In their early years, however, they produced a series of "cutout" forms, including tables, chairs, and case pieces, that were as interesting and satisfying as anything produced in this country. Some collectors still claim that these are a poor man's copies of English and Scottish precedents. They would do well to note how closely adaptive some of Gustav's own work was when he first designed Arts and Crafts wood.

L. and J. G. Stickley's work was initially regarded as purely imitative of their brother Gustav's. And, to a certain extent, this was true. It was their later furniture designs that provided a clear departure from the subsequent, watered-down offerings of Gustav. Their famous tall case clock, for example, designed by Peter Hansen in about 1910, was the best production model manufactured during the period. Even Gustav's powerful early version, produced nearly a decade earlier, lacked the power and grace of the L. and J. G. case.

L. AND J. G. STICKLEY TALL CASE CLOCK

Date Made: *ca 1910*

Dimensions: *80 ½" x 21 ½" x 13"*

Value: *$90,000–110,000*

Rare L. and J. G. Stickley tall case clock with beveled, overhanging top; large acid-etched copper face; glass-panel door with copper hardware; and brass works, weights, and pendulum. Excellent original finish, color, condition, and wood choice. Minor repair to front leg. Etched mark on face "L. and J. G. Stickley/Fayetteville NY/Handcraft."

While collectors' insistence on original condition wavered little, there was suddenly a greater understanding that the limitations of simple, straight-edged furniture offered many complexities to discriminating collectors.

The pottery world was also undergoing great change at this time. By about 1985, the interest in Victorian hand-painted pottery was clearly on the wane. For example, Rookwood Native American portraits began to drop in value in all but the best of cases. Only a few years earlier, the startling price of over $30,000

ROOKWOOD PLAQUE
Maker: *Grace Young*
Date Made: *1903*
Dimensions: *14¼" x 10"*
Value: *$80,000–90,000*

Standard-glaze Rookwood plaque of Chief High Hawk in headdress with breastplate and tomahawk. Made for the Louisiana Purchase Exposition in St. Louis, Missouri, 1904. Original frame.

had been paid for a large and striking profile of a brave in full headdress on a Rookwood pillow vase at a Christie's auction in New York City. While that pot just might bring that much or a bit more today, you could have purchased at full retail, the three best pieces of Grueby pottery for the same price. The Gruebys would be worth about $75,000 each today! The $30,000 Rookwood Native American marked the high point of the portrait market, and few Arts and Crafts collectors ever looked back.

Instead, the 1980s were a time when ceramics collectors focused on the best of the true Arts and Crafts potters. Grueby had always been a favored brand. Even Gustav Stickley—who was equally important for his guidance from the grave via fifteen years of *The Craftsman* magazine—used Grueby tiles in some of his furniture and often exhibited his work with Grueby pots adorning his furniture. The same philosophical chord ran through both companies, and their harmony was clear to all but the most obtuse. While prices for Grueby's work were fairly solid during the 1970s, collectors were able to buy the best examples inexpensively. It was at that time that the best collections of Grueby pottery were amassed.

It was probably a combination of higher prices and increased awareness that eventually led collectors to other great Arts and

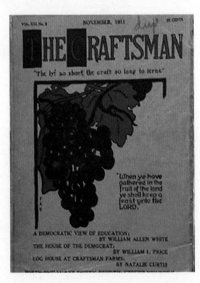

GUSTAV STICKLEY'S
CRAFTSMAN
MAGAZINE

AREQUIPA VASE

Date Made: *ca 1913*
Dimensions: *6" x 3¼"*
Value: *$6,000–7,000*

Unusual Arequipa vase embossed with branches of fruits and leaves in
pale matte blue on mottled indigo ground. Restoration to base chip.
Stamped "Arequipa/California/203/18/MA4."

Crafts potters. Fine, decorated Marblehead was very inexpensive at this time, as were the more obscure works by California potteries such as Arequipa, Grand Feu, and Frederick Rhead's studio in Santa Barbara.

The largest increase in collector interest, and pricing, was reserved for the best work of George Ohr. Ohr's pottery has remained one of those oddities that has, almost without exception, never lost value. It should not be surprising that the prices for Ohr's work mirrored the increased understanding of what he, and his pieces, were about.

When Ohr's pottery first hit the market in the early 1970s, there was virtually no way to interpret his craft. Unlike nearly every other period artisan, almost his entire body of work remained in family hands until New Jersey barber/ antiques dealer Jim Carpenter purchased his work, en masse, in 1970. Because of this, we did not see that broad dispersion back in the day that would have led to errant pieces surfacing at the flea markets and yard sales scattered across the country.

Instead, Ohr's pottery, once it became available, was nearly always in the hands of people who knew they were selling Ohr and knew something of its current value. Nevertheless, the man

and his pottery were so weird, so foreign, that his work begged reinterpretation as new information was released and better-informed people began to collect it.

For example, in 1975, Ohr was widely regarded as a folk potter, a homespun genius pursuing his own extravagant, if naive, vision. Within a decade, however, we came to see him as a modernist, the fly in the ointment of twentieth-century decorative art. He invented funk pottery, and he redefined the idea of functional shape in the process. Some of his teapots had lids fused to the bodies to render them unusable. Some of his vases couldn't possibly hold flowers. And he chose to leave nearly half of his pieces unglazed, complete in their raw form.

It was no small bit of luck that the New Jersey barber brought the hoard so close to Manhattan, the reigning center of the art world. By the 1980s, premier artists such as Andy Warhol and Jasper Johns avidly collected Ohr's work. Johns even included interpretations of Ohr vessels in his paintings and prints. Once the art intelligentsia discovered Ohr, the prices for his pieces grew exponentially.

I remember, at a Christie's auction in about 1982, a magnificent, if quirky, pink, blistered teapot. The body was misshapen, the handle kinked, the lid barely sitting in place, the glaze fragile and vulnerable to the touch. It was more sculptural than utile. It was

OHR TEAPOT
Maker: *George Ohr*
Date Made: *1895*
Dimensions: *8" x 7"*
Value: *$150,000–200,000*

Ohr teapot with a crumpled body and a kinked handle under a blister pink matte finish. Die-stamped mark. Private collection.

purchased for a then-record price of $6,600 by the notorious New York dealer Anthony Crispo, who would later do time for accessory to a murder.

The piece changed hands, selling through the Jordan-Volpe Gallery, where I worked at the time, for $10,000, ending up in the collection of a noted Princeton, New Jersey, collector. (As a footnote, though I'm getting ahead of the overall story here, I resold the piece in 1994 to a New York collector for $55,000. In 2001, I offered that collector $125,000 for the piece, having located a buyer at $150,000. His response was, "That's all?")

While stories — and there are many about George Ohr — say quite a bit about the market, they say equally as much about the leap of awareness that

DIRK VAN ERP DESK LAMP

Date Made: *1910*
Dimensions: *15" x 12"*
Value: *$100,000–125,000*

Early and rare Dirk Van Erp hammered-copper desk lamp with candlestick base, four riveted armatures, and four-paneled mica shade with vented cap. Single socket. Fine original patina and mica. Closed-box mark with "D'Arcy Gaw/Dirk Van Erp."

marked the 1980s and continued almost without let up through today. Just as more information and appreciation of the furniture of L. and J. G. Stickley was stoked by exorbitant Gustav Stickley prices, the same was true of much of the better art pottery.

Lighting also rode the wave of this interest, reaching the first of many crests in the 1980s. I recall my first great Dirk Van Erp lamp, purchased from a germinal San Francisco collector in 1984 for $14,000. Prior to that time, you could have bought just about the best Van Erp table lamps for $10,000 or less. That was soon to change.

DIRK VAN ERP TABLE LAMP

Date Made: *Pre-1915*
Dimensions: *24½" x 24"*
Value: *$150,000–200,000*

*Early large Van Erp table lamp
with a hammered-copper milk-can
base with four riveted arms below
four original sockets, ball chains,
and hammered cap, topped by a
four-panel copper-and-mica shade.
Excellent original mica and patina.
Rim of shade slightly out of round.
Stamped open-box windmill mark.
From the estate of the original owner.*

Dirk Van Erp, like many of the California masters, was under-stood only by a tight coterie of prescient California collectors. I suspect this resulted from a combination of having too little of it reach the East Coast prior to this time, and an abiding snobbery against things not from New York State. But those who knew something of Van Erp and his work understood that he could be to wrought copper what Ohr could be to clay.

His lamps were primarily sculptural, each from raised sheet copper, uniquely formed. Though they functioned as lamps, they were never easy to read by. The low-wattage bulbs diffused light through panels of mica schist, bathing an interior in a soft, moody glow. When people figured out these weren't lamps in the traditional sense, they began to seek them out hungrily.

Once collector interest in Van Erp's lamps blossomed across the country, increasing numbers of his lamps came to market and allowed the hands-on study of nuance that would eventually lead to scholarship. Initially, nearly all of his lamps were priced to within a few thousand dollars of each other. By 1985, that had abruptly changed.

The lamp I bought for $14,000 was a most unusual red warty example. I had not known, prior to that time, what "red warty" meant. It was a design born of process, where the raw hammer marks were imparted during the hammering and raising process.

The red was fused to the surface of the metal while being dipped into a rutile solution. Usually, the broader "warts" of the hammer were planished out, and the red removed or coated with a brown patina. Just as Ohr's pottery was initially preferred when it seemed "finished" with glazing, Van Erp was at first respected when handled in the more plentiful fashion.

But Van Erp's warty lamps and vases were soon understood to be his premier work, and the gap between the quotidian and the divine widened broadly in only a few short years. I sold that lamp almost immediately for $20,000 to another important New York dealer, Michael Carey, and the Van Erp market never looked back.

The high point of the 1980s was the Christie's auction of Gustav Stickley's own furniture that had been consigned by his son from Gustav's own home. Hollywood had only recently discovered the mysterious beauty of the material, and Barbara Streisand rocked that small world in 1988 by paying $335,000 for Gustav's family sideboard.

DIRK VAN ERP VASE
Date Made: *1910*
Dimensions: *5" x 6"*
Value: *$30,000–35,000*

"Curtained" copper bulbous vase with dimpled and folded sides covered in a rare original red finish. Windmill/San Francisco mark with partial "D'Arcy Gaw" visible.

The 1990s

The third decade of the revival of collecting Arts and Crafts objects and furniture started with a dull thud. After the soaring economics of the Reagan presidency, and the optimism generated by a fast and technically impressive war in Iraq, the nation settled into a lengthy recession during the Bush presidency. The recession put a temporary end to the madness as prices for, and interest in, Arts and Crafts went underground for several years. It was the worst time to collect Arts and Crafts, and it was the best time to collect Arts and Crafts. Let me explain why both of these statements are true, and how some collectors used these times to their advantage.

The first few years of the decade were a terrible time to buy Arts and Crafts because the prices were so low that many sellers were unmotivated to part with the things they already owned. If, for example, you knew that a particular Grueby vase was getting $2,000 a year before, you weren't going to be thrilled about accepting the $1,250 it was suddenly worth.

While some people may have needed to sell the pot at any price, most dealers and collectors chose to wait things out. As a result, the majority of "known" pieces, or those that had already been rescued from attics and garage sales, were staying put. If anything, the people who already owned the goods were selling mostly from the bottom of their collections, saving the best for a better time.

A down market also meant less funding for shows and exhibitions, less incentive for new research and publishing, and fewer buyers entering the marketplace to start new collections. With the exception of the ill-fated George Ohr exhibition at the Crafts Museum in New York City (I'll explain this in the Ohr Pottery chapter), there was relatively little high-end promotion happening.

What was interesting was that, even with the economy as bad as it was, there were still collectors buying and paying record prices. These instances just happened less frequently during this time.

The reason the first three years of the decade were a great

L. AND J. G. STICKLEY
CHIFFONIER
Date Made: *1910*
Dimensions: *48" x 40" x 19"*
Value: *$7,000–10,000*

*L. and J. G. Stickley chiffonier
with two paneled doors and metal
pulls. Refinished, replaced lockset.
Branded "Work of..." left drawer.*

time to buy Arts and Crafts was because prices were lower overall than they had been since the mid-1980s. Additionally, there
was more information available to buyers than at any other time.
In short, people buying Arts and Crafts had better taste and more
knowledge behind them than ever before, and prices were, almost
without exception, cheaper than they had been in a decade.

While it was true that less was coming to market, it was also
true that, when it did, people with a little money to spend had
an excellent chance of acquiring quality Arts and Crafts. Back in
the mid- to late 1980s, for example, there was great furniture
and lighting at four major specialty auctions. Museums, movie
stars, recording artists, and tycoons were all slugging it out with
the high-end dealers in the field. Yet, only a few years later there

MARBLEHEAD VASE

Maker: *Hannah Tutt*
Date Made: *1910*
Dimensions: *6¼" x 4"*
Value: *$110,000–130,000*

Rare and important Marblehead ovoid vase, carved with tall stylized flowers in umber, black, and cream on a speckled matte green ground. Impressed ship mark/incised "HT."

often was only one bidder competing against a reserve, or seller's minimum. Buyers with money had their pick of the market, and some of the best collections currently in existence were either built or filled out at this time.

What were collectors buying? Advanced collectors focused once again on high-end pieces in mint, original condition. But instead of looking only for Gustav Stickley furniture or Robineau pottery, their interest was more design oriented and included top pieces by Rohlfs, L. and J. G. Stickley, Limbert, Van Erp, Marblehead, Ohr, and early Newcomb College pottery. Even Grueby pottery, which had the distinction of being highly regarded yet stagnant in price, started to garner higher prices.

On the other hand, there was suddenly a broadened interest in furniture and ceramics by secondary makers, such as the furniture of Stickley Brothers and Lifetime, and the pottery of Hampshire, Walley, and better matte-glazed pottery of Newcomb College. It was clear that the look and the philosophy of Arts and Crafts had taken hold of contemporary collectors, and while not all of them wanted or could afford the very best, they were nevertheless interested in less-expensive quality pieces. These items were very inexpensive in the early 1990s, especially in comparison to first-tier work.

For example, even though Grueby pottery was still underpriced, a Grueby piece would sell for $1,500 while a comparable piece of Hampshire would bring only about $300. Once again, the high prices of the favored brands encouraged a greater understanding of lesser but still quality period goods.

There was also a growing interest in California Arts and Crafts, the majority of which were not Greene and Greene. Just as the Arts and Crafts movement took an extra decade

GRUEBY VASE

Date Made: *1905*
Dimensions: *11" x 9¼"*
Value: *$50,000–60,000*

Exceptional Grueby Kendrick vase with seven tooled and applied handles alternating with two rows of incised and folded leaves on a double gourd-shaped base, covered in a rare, organic matte mustard glaze. One of three ochre Kendrick handled vases known. Horizontal body line near base and a few minor flakes to edges. Stamped Faience mark. From the estate of the original owner.

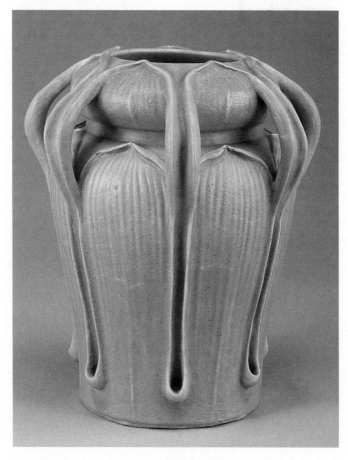

HANS JAUCHEN PLAQUE

Date Made: *ca 1910*
Dimensions: *24" x 17¼"*
Value: *$10,000–15,000*

Fine and rare Hans Jauchen repoussé copper wall plaque depicting two tall trees in a landscape. Original dark patina. Signed "H. Jauchen/Sculptor/ S.F. Cal" lower right.

GRAND FEU VASE

Date Made: *ca 1916*
Dimensions: *8¼" x 4½"*
Value: *$1,000–1,500*

Fine, rare, and large Grand Feu baluster vase covered in mottled celadon glaze on red ground. Restored five-inch C-shaped line. Stamped "GRAND FEU/L.A. CAL./15."

to fully reach California, and just as the bulk of contemporary collectors were centered in points east, the 1990s was a time when some of the greatest collections in America were being formed on the West Coast. It is safe to say that the passion and money of California collectors were primarily responsible for sustaining the market during these hard times and funding its resurgence beginning around 1994 or 1995.

These new collectors were cut from a different cloth, however. While great pieces of Gustav Stickley furniture and Grueby pottery might find their way into California homes, these collectors were as inclined to buy a great lamp by Elizabeth Burton or Albert Berry, a handcrafted pot by Frederick Rhead from

BROUWER VASE

Maker: *Theopolous Brouwer*
Date Made: *ca 1910*
Dimensions: *5¼" x 5½"*
Value: *$750–1,000*

Brouwer bulbous vase with closed-in rim. Flame-painted in amber, orange, yellow, and brown. A couple of minor flecks to rim and base. Incised flame.

Arequipa, or a high-fired Grand Feu vase.

One of the early signs of what was to come during the 1990s occurred during my New York City auction of the Rosalie Berberian pottery collection in February of 1993. Even though this was still a time when prices for Arts and Crafts were very soft, a number of records, which still stand, were set at that sale. What is noteworthy is that these records were set for esoteric, non-mainstream works such as Dedham ($45,000), Brouwer ($27,500), Wannopee ($11,000), and Jervis ($16,500). It might have been regarded as a market blip at that time, a case of extreme pricing for closet favorites that had been ensconced in a famous collection. But, in retrospect, it is evident that the collectors had a deep understanding of great Arts and Crafts material, as well as deep pocketbooks. For example, Yale University, buying for their art museum's permanent collection, was a major player at that sale.

DEDHAM VASE

Maker: *Hugh Robertson*
Date Made: *ca 1900*
Dimensions: *10" x 7"*
Value: *$5,000–7,000*

Large and exceptional Dedham experimental bulbous vase, covered in a fine, frothy oxblood glaze. Two small nicks to rim. Incised "Dedham Pottery" in script and "HR."

LIFETIME CHINA CABINET
Date Made: *1910*
Dimensions: *58" x 39" x 15"*
Value: *$3,000–4,000*

Lifetime two-door china cabinet with single glass pane to doors and sides, two interior shelves, and lower drawer. Hammered-copper hardware. Good original finish. Decal.

By mid-decade, the market was picking up speed, fueled by the burgeoning economy of the Clinton era. New collectors were establishing markets for nearly anything Arts and Crafts, decorating with a "look" as much as collecting for authenticity. Even neophytes who had little understanding of the period were buying reproductions in quantity. It was definitely hip to have Arts and Crafts pieces in your home.

It was Gustav in the '70s, L. and J. G. in the '80s, and Lifetime in the early '90s. The late '90s was the time of well-designed (and sometimes poorly designed) generic furniture and reproductions. European Arts and Crafts was also gaining in popularity in America's press to find the best quality for the money.

In ceramics, the better Rookwood production pieces were recording all-time high prices, and undecorated Marblehead, plain Grueby, and even plain Hampshire were selling briskly. The biggest increase was seen in lighting, with Van Erp lamps setting record after record, and generic period lighting bringing thousands of dollars for anything that approximated wrought copper or dark-stained wood.

It was clear, by the end of the millennium, that America's interest had gone from curiosity, to fad, to mainstay. The market continues to sort itself out, directed by a nationwide foundation of collectors and dealers who have warmed to this simple esthetic. There is no denying that America's interest in Arts and Crafts is no longer a passing fancy.

This book, then, is not for the beginning collector, or at least not for the beginner who intends to stay one long.

ENGLISH ARTS AND CRAFTS LANTERN

Date Made: *ca 1900*
Dimensions: *18" x 6¼" sq.*
Value: *$3,000–4,000 (lantern only)*

Fine English Arts and Crafts silver-plated lantern with cutout and embossed hearts. Inset with four glass panes, encasing beaded floral motif in green, red, and amber. Complete with hanging chain. Deterioration and loss to beadwork. Unmarked.

Arts and Crafts Pottery

I THINK IT'S BEST TO KEEP THINGS SIMPLE now that we're getting into the meat of this book. Each of the following pottery chapters talks briefly about a particular company's approach to ceramic design, what collectors have traditionally preferred, and what I think you should be looking for. I also discuss the impact of damage on value, what types of flaws you should avoid, and what distress offers the best chance for a reasonable price.

Criteria for Pottery Chapter Entries

From about 1875 until about 1925, there were over 200 American companies producing American art pottery. Yet, I cover fewer than twenty in this chapter. There are a number of good reasons for my selections and exclusions, which in and of themselves will be useful to you.

To begin with, at least half of these companies worked primarily in styles that were not Arts and Crafts. From the Victorian lines of the Dallas and Cincinnati art potteries, to the Art Deco bent of Cowan, many of these firms had little in common with the companies I've selected for this chapter other than their production of decorative pottery.

Next, some of these companies produced wares with design elements from several eras. The Roseville Pottery, for example, made Victorian lines such as Royal Dark, Art Nouveau ware such as Fudjiyama, and even commercial pottery of Deco and Moderne influence. Their Della Robbia line is one of my personal favorites and arguably Arts and Crafts in look if not spirit. But, because too little of what Roseville produced was genuinely Arts and Crafts, I chose not to cover them in this guide.

On the other hand, the Rookwood Pottery also made pottery for a long period of time, encompassing an array of styles similar to those at the Roseville Pottery, yet they are included. I made

this exception because, while the Arts and Crafts was only a pregnant stop in their long line of ceramic production, they were more committed to the era. Instead of offering only a single line, such as Roseville's Della Robbia, Rookwood had carved mattes, painted mattes, incised mattes, and sculpted Z-line pieces. These pieces were often derivative of work by other American or European artists and companies. Nevertheless, the Rookwood Pottery typically created art pottery of the highest order and deserve at least limited coverage here.

Finally, I felt quality was an essential issue. While even some of the minor Arts and Crafts–era companies produced some very good work, this book is a guide for the advanced collector. For example, though the studio at North Dakota School of Mines saw the production of some exceptional and original art pottery, most was student work that has insufficient merit for placement in a book on connoisseurship.

In the end, I had to draw the line somewhere, so I chose to include only what was consistently the best of what the Arts and Crafts had to offer in American decorative ceramics. The companies that follow established and maintained that position. They are all worthy of your consideration today.

Arequipa Pottery

THERE ARE THREE DISTINCTLY DIFFERENT TYPES OF
AREQUIPA POTTERY, ranging from some of the best ware made
during the Arts and Crafts period to a fairly boring undecorated
ceramic that inspires little serious interest beyond the mark on
the bottom. The Arequipa Pottery was an Arts and Crafts experi-
ment in which patients at a sanatorium were instructed in handi-
crafts as part of their convalescence program. For the most part,
the pots look amateurish.

On the other hand, English-American master Frederick H.
Rhead taught and decorated at the sanatorium for about two
years from 1910 to 1912, also known as the Rhead period. Pots
made during this time are of primary interest. Bear in mind that
Arequipa mostly employed matte finishes. Pots, usually eight
inches or less in height, were both thrown and molded.

Rhead Period

Frederick Rhead was one of the most important figures in
pre–World War I decorated ceramics in America. That he was
willing to take a position at such a small and remote studio after
being one of the big guns at the Roseville Pottery in Zanesville,
Ohio, says much about him and his maturation as a ceramist.

This is not to say that everything Rhead did while at Arequipa,
nor that all the pots made under his supervision, are particularly
noteworthy. In fact, the majority of Arequipa pots, regardless of
who made them or when they were made, are fairly boring.

Look for pieces bearing a Rhead period mark, of which there
are at least two variations. The first and most common is a
painted blue image of a pot sitting beneath a tree, on a white
ground, and often under a glossy, transparent circle. The second
is the same designation cut sharply into the clay with the thin,
sure strokes of a potter's tool.

Date Made: *1913–1915*
Dimensions: *11" tall*
Value: *$70,000–80,000*

*Frederick Rhead in squeezebag with iris blossoms and green leaves on a
satin black ground. This piece is particularly noteworthy because of the
quality of decoration, the amount of surface covered by the decoration, and
its overall size.*

Date Made: *1912*
Dimensions: *3" tall*
Value: *$2,300–2,800*

Arequipa cabinet vase with multi-color slip trail, or squeezebag, work. The best examples decorated in this style have designs that are both delineated with slip trail and have enamel colors inside the outlined areas.

The best of these pots were decorated using a squeezebag, or slip trail, technique, where colored slip was applied in much the same way a baker decorates a cake. Most of these pots (and they are quite rare) have a stylized leaf design and occasionally berries in relief in a narrow band restricted mainly to the top rim. Even better are pieces where a colorful, glossy enamel fills in the negative space within the tube-lined outlines.

But the very best—of which there are precious few examples— have vessel surfaces that are entirely incorporated into the design. Often, this might mean that arching squeezebag lines delineate stylized leaves from the bottom half of the pot. The upper part of the ceramic sur- face is decorated with wild flowers in multicolors, often with glossy enamels filling the insides of each outline.

Date Made: *post-1914*
Dimensions: *13½" tall*
Value: *$3,000-4,000*

Pieces made during the Solon period, after about 1914, are uneven in quality. This vase is one of those rare exceptions. Unusually large and heavily deco- rated, the piece is covered with a fine crackled glaze that allows the clay to show through. This piece is also important because it presages the studio pottery movement in America, which was to follow after the First World War.

I've seen fewer than ten such pieces in the past three decades, including ones with designs of tulips, iris blossoms, and California poppies. The last of these to reach the market, with colorful irises, sold in one of our sales for $72,000. It may be the last one we ever see. Needless to say, minor damage will have little impact on the pricing of such pieces. They deserve such respect.

The Solon Period

After Rhead's departure, the noted ceramist Albert Solon became head of the ceramics department at Arequipa. This was the last gasp for the firm which, like most of this country's art potteries, failed to survive beyond World War I. While pieces Rhead decorated are difficult to find, Solon's pots are considerably rarer. As of this writing, I've handled only two examples that clearly show his hand.

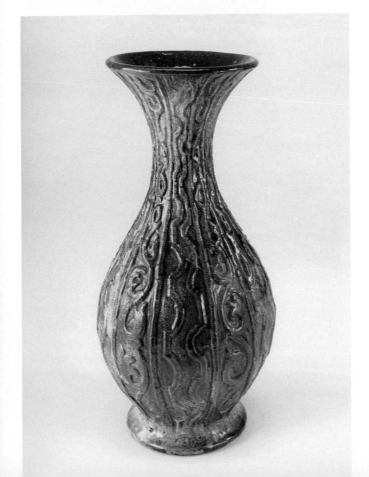

Solon was known for many things, primarily the introduction of crackled glazes. When used in tandem with the gentle modeling of the surface, these pieces can be quite lovely, speaking more of what art pottery was to become after the first World War. The last piece I saw was a tall vase modeled with a stylized floral design from top to bottom. It was covered with a fine, pale green–blue crackle glaze. That it was difficult to sell for $3,000 says more about the reticence of the current market than the quality or scarcity of the ware. Solon's work, at least the best of it, is a bargain.

Date Made: *ca 1915*
Dimensions: *6" tall*
Value: *$3,500–4,500*

Though probably a student's pot rather than that of a teacher, this piece is still relatively ambitious in design and execution.

The Rest of It

Most of the Arequipa you're likely to see are smallish vases of bulbous form with either molded decoration of flowers, or no embossed work at all. These are often covered with dark matte finishes of green or blue. You'll sometimes see a few high-gloss glazes. These are rare and have some value. I do not mean to denigrate them entirely by stating that they are unworthy of your consideration. But, once again, this book is for advanced collectors and, if you're looking to acquire the best from this company, you are better off avoiding them entirely.

Post-Rhead pieces are marked with one of several die-stamped company marks, all of which say "Arequipa" in one fashion or another. Even minor damage on such examples will severely reduce their value.

Date Made: *ca 1914*
Dimensions: *5" tall*
Value: *$2,300–2,800*

This is another unusual piece of Arequipa. The technique would suggest it was made after Rhead's departure from the studio. However, since Rhead favored rich black glazes, it was likely made during his tenure there. Nevertheless, the sharpness of the carving shows a stronger hand than most examples.

Brouwer Pottery

BROUWER POTTERY HAS BEEN A RELATIVELY RARE COMMODITY OVER THE YEARS, but enough comes to market, and the quality level is sufficiently high, to warrant inclusion here. Frankly, the more I read about Theopolous Brouwer's work, the more confused I am about what glazes he employed and the techniques he pioneered. Fortunately, if you rely more on your eye than your brain, Brouwer is fairly easy to assess.

For the most part, Brouwer used the fire of an open kiln face to paint iridescent colors, mostly in gold, brown, and orange tones, on the sides of relatively thin, low-fire, molded, or hurriedly thrown pots. There are many variations in form and size, and a limited number of curiosities with applied decoration. But 90 percent of the Brouwer ware you'll see will be six inches or less in height; gold, orange, or brown in color; lightweight; and clearly marked.

Date Made: *ca 1910-1915*
Dimensions: *13" tall*
Value: *$9,000-11,000*

Tall and exceptional Brouwer vase with a rich, dark metallic drip ending unevenly over a vibrant, fire-painted flambé. Brouwer normally lavished a great deal of attention on taller pieces.

Date Made: *1910–1915*
Dimensions: *13" tall*
Value: *$9,000–11,000*

Tall, ribbed Brouwer vase with gold fire painting. The body of these vases are uniformly light in weight. Like Hugh Robertson at Dedham, Brouwer seemed more interested in the glazes than in the pottery itself.

Glazes

You're likely to find as much poorly fired Brouwer ware as you are pieces with rich, even iridescence. Look for pieces with overall brilliance in color and a rich nacreous sheen above the surface. Generally, the more color, the better.

Date Made: *1910–1915*
Dimensions: *13" tall*
Value: *$11,000–13,000*

Exceptional, tall vase with a thick, deep metallic glaze on top of a rich, fire-painted base. These large vases often doubled as lamp bases, with delineated circles at the centers of their bases, which could easily be knocked out to accommodate metal fittings.

Date Made: *1910–1915*
Dimensions: *6" tall*
Value: *$900–1,100*

All Brouwer is rare, but this is an example of a poorly fired piece of fire-painted ware. While the color is consistent with most other pieces, this one lacks the iridescence and intensity of better work.

Pieces that have a second contrasting glaze are rare, and the few examples to surface have been memorable. One such piece had a thick, creamy layer around the top shoulder. Another had a textured, deep bronze drip over a more standard, golden orange ground. It seemed that Brouwer knew when he was working on something special because nearly all such pieces were larger in size, topping out at about twelve inches in height.

Applied Decoration

A self-taught ceramic master, Brouwer was a renaissance man whose skills also included sculpture, architecture, and painting. Some of his best pieces are not only covered with his marvelous glazes but are further embellished with applied decoration.

His most common decorations are leaves and flower forms. These, too, are usually found on larger, more important pieces. I have seen several smaller pieces with applied decoration, but these are in the minority. Rarer still are vases with applied creatures such as snakes.

Brouwer pottery is usually smallish in size, relying on squat bulbous vases under six inches in height. The clay is very thin and light, and the firing appears to have been at low temperatures. It is reasonable to expect that Brouwer pieces will have at least some minor damage, usually nicks or small chips around the top rim. Expect minor damage on major pieces to reduce value by no more than 10 percent.

Brouwer ware is nearly always marked with at least one of several designations, including the hand-incised *Brouwer* or *Middle Lane Pottery* and stylized whale jawbones.

Date Made: *1910–1915*
Dimensions: *6" tall*
Value: *$1,800–2,200*

A very typical piece of Brouwer flame ware. Notice how the iridized colors look as though they were flames licking the sides of the pot. They were.

Date Made: *1910–1915*
Dimensions: *5" tall*
Value: *$2,300–2,500*

Perhaps one in thirty pieces of Brouwer flame ware was decorated with applied designs. In this case, a stylized leaf in a contrasting color has been added.

Dedham Pottery

WHEN MOST PEOPLE THINK OF DEDHAM POTTERY, they usually envision crackleware pieces with blue border designs of bunnies and flowers. While such pieces might be the best hand-made dinnerware made in America during and after the Arts and Crafts period, they have little in common with the high-end decorative art covered in this book. In fact, this crackleware is important only in that the Dedham factory was able to stay afloat due to its commercial viability. Dedham organic, experimental hollowware is of far more interest to us.

Hugh Robertson was a dedicated art potter and, like most of his kind, was far more successful in creating beautiful pots than he was in running a business. He discovered his crackled glazes by mistake, and their development ultimately led to the production of his popular dinnerware. On the verge of bankruptcy, he was convinced by his financial backers to produce dinnerware as the company's mainstay. Money from the sale of dinnerware allowed Robertson to continue with his glaze experiments for several more decades, well into the twentieth century.

Robertson's work with glazes began before the formation of the Dedham Pottery, while he was potting in association with his brothers and his father at the Chelsea Keramic Art Works in the 1870s and 1880s. I have chosen not to cover pieces from this period, even though the quality level was at least as good and usually better than other pieces covered here. Chelsea pieces usually have more to do with Victorian influences than Arts and Crafts. Also, it is not clear exactly who made each experimentally glazed piece at Chelsea, since artists never signed such pieces.

Robertson's preoccupation with glazes resulted in a ceramic tunnel vision unlike any other in this country. His best vases were usually clumsily thrown, unimaginative in shape, and often had numerous firing and glazing flaws. They were, in fact, little more than canvases for him to work his peculiar magic.

Maker: *H. C. Robertson*
Date Made: *ca 1900*
Dimensions: *6½" tall*
Value: *$3,000–4,000*

Fine Dedham volcanic vase with multicolored flambé over a crackled ground. While nearly all of Robertson's work in this style could be considered experimental, the ones masking blue and white crackled decoration are the most extreme.

In spite of how well glazed some of his pieces are, Robertson's masterworks are heavily outnumbered by boring pieces covered with thin, glossy, apple green and murky brown flambés. Dedham experimental ware is fairly rare, and their best work was achieved perhaps 5 percent of the time. Following are guidelines to help you distinguish what quality Dedham looks like.

Maker: *H. C. Robertson*
Date Made: *ca 1900*
Dimensions: *10" tall*
Value: *$3,500–4,500*

Large baluster form vase, more graceful in form than most, with a rich, feathered, oxblood flambé.

Forms

As stated earlier, Robertson's shape selection was predictable and mostly unmemorable.

He favored thick vases with slightly bulbous bottoms and slightly tapered sides. They were roughly thrown and often show deep firing fissures through the bottom and tight firing cracks to the top rim. The bottoms are also heavy, as though he did not care enough to raise the wet clay into the sides while throwing the pot.

Maker: *H. C. Robertson*
Date Made: *ca 1910*
Dimensions: *6¼" tall*
Value: *$2,300–2,700*

The form of this bulbous Dedham vase is more typical and less graceful than some of the other examples. The four-color flambé favors browns over reds. While still a fine piece of American art pottery, it is clearly a cut below the previous baluster vase.

It probably makes more sense to think of his pots the way he did: as a ceramic surface on which his best glazes could gather and play. For this reason, the larger and broader the pot, the better. Forget about pitchers, teapots, and the like. He certainly did. The most common and successful form Robertson used was an ovoid vase about eight inches in height.

It is worth noting that he produced a disproportionate number of cabinet, or small, vases. Many of these were probably glaze test pieces and often bear some of his most successful glazes. While such examples will seldom be ranked among his master-pieces, they should not be automatically discounted.

Glazes

Robertson is most famous for his "rediscovery" of the ancient Chinese *sang de boeuf*, or oxblood glaze. He described the perfect oxblood as having the color of "fresh arterial blood." There is no question this was his most important finish. He produced it in numerous combinations, with varying degrees of success. Bear in mind that this glaze was achieved by firing a celadon green glaze in an oxygen reduction kiln, the minerals in the green becoming red in the process. This is an important fact because many oxblood vases are either red with patches of green, or green with patches of red.

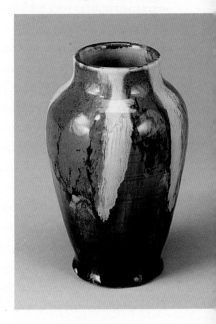

Maker: *H. C. Robertson*
Date Made: *ca 1910*
Dimensions: *7 ¼" tall*
Value: *$1,800–2,200*

Not all Dedham ware has to be red to be beautiful. This short baluster vase makes use of a weak, thin, apple green back-ground glaze to accentuate the dynamic flambé overglaze.

Maker: *H. C. Robertson*
Date Made: *ca 1910*
Dimensions: *9" tall*
Value: *$2,300–2,700*

Another interesting non-red vase, though not as successful as the previous short baluster vase.

Maker: *H. C. Robertson*
Date Made: *ca 1900*
Dimensions: *5½" tall*
Value: *$2,500–3,500*

This simple pot has an excellent oxblood glazing.

The best oxblood glaze examples are mostly covered with rich, gloppy red finishes with gold-luster overglazing. Textures range from smooth, to orange peel, to volcanic. As a rule, the more active the glaze, the better the pot.

Better still are pieces where additional bright colors were employed, including navy blue; thick, brilliant green; gun metal; and even dripping, crackled whites. While red always predominates visually on better pieces, it may be limited to only a fraction of the vase's surface, acting in tandem with other finishes.

Finally, texture is of critical importance. Remember that this is an organic, experimental ware, gutsy and powerful. Smooth, even finishes are good as far as they go, but advanced collectors prefer blisters and volcanic flourishes. Once again, the more active the surface, the better the pot.

The best piece I have ever seen, which is currently in the Yale University Art Museum collection, is about eleven inches tall by about six inches across. It is covered primarily with an active red flambé, splotched with deep green, royal blue, and dashes of gun metal.

Damage has relatively minor impact on pricing, especially considering that there are often numerous manufacturing issues on many pieces. Tight lines at the rim or base, especially on that one in a hundred masterpiece, will likely reduce worth by no more than 20 percent. However, a large chip or chunk out of the top rim will severely reduce value. Frankly, if you're fortunate enough to find one of these with anything less than serious damage, you should buy it.

Robertson signed the vast majority of these pieces. It's worth noting that it's much better to have a great example with no artist signature, or that of an associate, than a Robertson-signed piece of even good quality.

Maker: *H. C. Robertson*
Date Made: *ca 1900*
Dimensions: *5" tall*
Value: *$1,800—2,200*

This piece has a more brilliant and dynamic glazing.

Fulper Pottery

FULPER POTTERY IS MY PERSONAL FAVORITE, probably because it's local to where I grew up. As a child, I once stood in front of the huge Stangl kilns that picked up where Fulper left off. Fulper is one of the more misunderstood American art potteries, perhaps because it had the misfortune of lasting too long.

It's difficult to either criticize or highly praise much of this company's earlier work, which was made prior to World War I. Fulper established a market for strong, somewhat mass-produced art pottery with superior, hand-applied glazes adorning molded forms. Fulper was determined to stay in business after World War I had marked the end to the Arts and Crafts movement and many of the decorative art companies under that umbrella. Fulper persevered until the Great Depression before reincarnating as the Stangl Pottery.

Three of Fulper's early marks, including a Vasekraft-era label. In addition to these, there is also a slightly later, vertically incised mark that is often found on their better work. While pieces with other later marks might occasionally be special, most of their great work bears one of these designations.

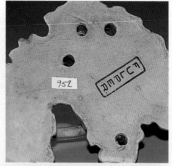

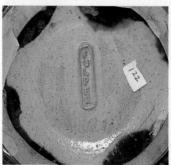

Date Made: *ca 1915*
Dimension: *12" tall*
Value: *$9,000–11,000*

*Tall corseted vase with exceptional copperdust crystalline glaz-
ing. Even back in the early days of collecting art pottery, this
was regarded as one of the Fulper's signature pieces. It shows
a combination of powerful form and classic Fulper glaze.*

Survival meant compromise, and each of these two disastrous
eras—World War I and the Depression—marked noticeable
changes in the company's output. In short, most of Fulper's best
work was produced prior to 1915, relatively little of it through
the mid-1920s, and almost none of it after that point.

I would advise you to focus almost entirely on pieces bearing
Fulper's earliest marks, all of which are shown here. But do not
exclude their entire later output from your collection because
the kiln is a funny thing. Even in its dotage, the company came
up with the occasional gem. As you develop your eye, you should
learn to trust what it says is beautiful; don't be limited merely to
a marking system. That said, especially if you're just beginning
to collect Fulper pottery, focusing on early pieces will do far
more good than harm.

Early Work

Fulper's early work can be more or less divided into two styles: Arts and Crafts and Oriental. The former is typified by severe or angular forms, the latter often by the curving lines of Chinese and Korean ceramics. In an odd way, Fulper often seems at its best when either very large or very small. The market has traditionally paid well for pieces over twelve inches tall or under four inches.

Date Made: *ca 1915*
Dimension: *10" tall*
Value: *$500–700*

A somewhat modest piece of Fulper with an exceptional green-and-black cucumber matte finish. Even beginning collectors can buy pieces with advanced elements for moderate prices.

Date Made: *ca 1915*
Dimension: *12" tall*
Value: *$2,500–3,500*

Some of the company's best early work was influenced by Asian antecedents. This lobed, footed vase is covered in an intense, mirrored, Cat's Eye flambé.

I would suggest starting by collecting middle-sized works, those averaging about six to eight inches in height. I understand that this might sound a bit silly, but most of their early vases in that size range can be had for under $500, and there is little other American ware that consistently offers such quality for such a value. Fulper is one of the least expensive of America's potteries (entry levels for quality pieces from other companies are well above $1,000). By comparison, taller vases usually begin at $1,000 and can easily reach two to three times that amount for pieces that are less than great.

Date Made: *ca 1910*
Dimension: *13" tall*
Value: *$4,000–5,000*

The cattail vase, another important piece of early Fulper in the Arts and Crafts style, almost always has a deep green matte finish.

Date Made: *ca 1910*
Dimension: *4" tall*
Value: *$900–1,100*

A marvelous cabinet-sized bell pepper vase with a three-color metallic flambé ending in a microcrystalline brown matte.

Similarly, Fulper produced a handsome series of cabinet and bud vases that display their best glazes. These gems have been a collecting favorite, perhaps because inch for inch they are the best hollowware this company fired. Often, a three-to-four-inch pot brings as much as a vase two to three times its size, even with the same glaze combination.

I certainly understand that there are large vases that bring well under $1,000, while cabinet pieces bring $200 or less. Usually dull and lifeless, with little color variation, these pieces don't deserve higher prices. And there are seven-inch forms, rare and/or covered with extraordinary glazing, that have brought $2,000 or more. If we're going to grouse about exceptions to the rule, we're not going to get anywhere. I'm suggesting only that the best value for Fulper ware is available for mid-sized pieces from the early period with at least moderately interesting glazing.

Glazes

Fulper pottery is much more about the glazing than it is about form, though worthy pieces share a quality combination of both. But a simple shape with a great glaze will almost always bring more than a great shape with a boring glaze.

Fulper had only about two dozen glazes in their repertoire, though they blended these on most vases to create an exponential number of variations. Most Fulper finishes were occasionally used alone, and all of them were mixed into flambés at some point. The best of them individually are Copperdust, Mirrored Black, Cat's Eye, and Flemington Green (which is actually a flambé of black and green). And many of their best vases bear either these glazes or a combination of these with other glazes.

On the other hand, avoid most pieces glazed in only one matte finish with the exception of brown. Simple red mattes, unaided by striations of other colors, can be pretty dull. Fulper would have been better off without their medium blue matte. Even their purple matte finish, unless assisted by the intermodulation of creams and soft blues, or bulwarked with a gloppy texture, is unexciting.

Finally, texture is an important component of Fulper glazing. Most pieces have a smooth surface, regardless of whether it is matte or glossy. The best Fulper often provides some textural contrast in the form of clumping or streaking, especially where two different glazes meet.

Date Made: *1915*
Dimension: *13" tall*
Value: *$1,800–2,200*

Some of the firm's best pots are glazed not only in contrasting colors but in diverse textures as well. Note how this rich ivory gloss ends in drips over an intense mirrored brown.

Shapes

Pre–World War I Fulper pottery has a lot in common with Chinese food. It's as hard to get a great meal as it is a bad one since most Chinese fare is usually a safe bet for a decent repast. Similarly, if you were to buy ten early pieces of Fulper in the six-to-nine-inch range, unless you were terribly unlucky or unimaginably fortunate, eight of the pieces would likely be solid, handsome examples, one of them dreary, and one of them well above average for the form and glaze. I hope this book can help you improve this average.

Shape is the most difficult thing to describe, and I rely on a few of our archival photos to illustrate some of the company's better forms. However, you are the only one who can determine what you want to live with and collect. But I like these.

Date Made: *ca 1910*
Dimension: *12" tall*
Value: *$2,300–2,800*

A great Chinese translation bulbous vase with a dynamic mirrored black and mirrored blue crystalline combination. Fulper often used the same glazes on the same forms, so it is necessary to carefully assess how well fired each example is.

Date Made: *ca 1910*
Dimension: *5" tall*
Value: *$500–700*

In the years prior to 1915, Fulper made an assortment of cabinet vases that are handsome both in form and glazing. This rare double gourd vase shows a rich brown- and-green crystalline flambé.

Date Made: *ca 1910*
Dimension: *7" tall (15" in diameter!)*
Value: *$1,800–2,200*

Some Fulper forms were available in three graduated sizes. This huge low bowl is fairly unmemorable in smaller versions. However, the larger size is almost always accompanied by exceptional glazing.

Condition

Unlike Grueby, Fulper is repeatable, molded ware. While each piece was rendered unique by the vagaries of the kiln, you can almost always find the exact form with some variation in nearly every glaze. Because of this, collectors are less willing to accept Fulper with more than minimal damage unless the piece is a great example.

Much Fulper ware shows grinding flakes around the base, which are little pieces of glazing that flecked off when the foot ring was ground flat at the factory so the ware would sit evenly on a tabletop. These are the sort of flaws that should not bother you in the least, unless they are terribly obvious from the side. Drill holes are another "limited" defect in that they do not interfere with the beauty of the pot and will not worsen with age.

But cracked Fulper, pieces with chunks broken off, or those with serious firing defects should be avoided unless the price is 10 percent of normal value.

Markings

Listed on page 64 are the marks you're most likely to find on Fulper pottery. Once again, while the pottery made some ghastly pottery early on and the occasional gem during their later period, stick with pieces whose markings date before 1920.

Date Made: *ca 1910*
Dimension: *24" tall*
Value: *$4,000–5,000*

An extraordinary and massive piece of early Fulper. Perhaps only three of these have surfaced over the last three decades. Even though these are molded pots, they are worth collecting with anything less than serious damage.

Grand Feu Pottery

GRAND FEU WAS ONE OF THOSE QUIRKY CALIFORNIA COMPANIES working in the Los Angeles area from 1912 until about 1917. *Grand feu* means "high fire." Having a hard clay body, these pieces were able to withstand extreme kiln temperatures, which resulted in the formation of deep and often intense glazing.

Grand Feu was mostly a one-trick pony. They used a limited number of rich glazes, usually alone, and occasionally in flambé. But what an excellent trick it was. It seems odd that in spite of the abundance of rich clays found in the Golden State, many of the California companies from the art pottery period made primarily small pots. Grand Feu was no exception. Grand Feu pieces that measure over five inches tall are very rare.

Date Made: *ca 1915*
Dimension: *8" diameter*
Value: *$3,500–4,500*

Classic Grand Feu closed-bowl form with intense, high-fire glazing.

Glazes

Glaze consideration is of paramount importance in assessing Grand Feu pottery because there was simply never any hand tooling of designs. I have seen one example with stylized, cut-through reticulations. This is about as extravagant as Grand Feu gets. Grand Feu is all about glazing, and the best pieces should be flamboyantly finished or finely nuanced.

Most of the Grand Feu that has surfaced to date is glazed either in semigloss or matte brown or green tones. These are fine, as far as they go, but rarely do these examples comprise the best of this firm's production.

Better glazes, alone or in combination with others, are more textured and/or colorful. For example, there are a few pieces with a drizzled light and dark blue flambé, offering some texture and great contrast. Another important piece, which is often on display at the Los Angeles County Museum of Art, is a tall pot with three different gloss flambés playing over its surface.

Date Made: *ca 1915*
Dimension: *6" tall*
Value: *$2,000–3,000*

A handsome, if relatively unexciting, piece glazed in mission matte brown. Even the firm's sedate glazes were of the highest order, a reason some aficionados consider Grand Feu one of the best of the American art potteries.

Date Made: *ca 1915*
Dimension: *7" tall*
Value: *$9,000–11,000*

Another example of high-fire glazing, showing a good mix of contrasting colors on a hard, almost porcelain ground.

Around 1994, a small collection of Grand Feu pottery was found in a house sale in the California mountains. A long-lost family member must have assembled and protected this collection, even though several pieces were literally salvaged from a trash can. Nearly every example from this cache was glazed with finishes that had not been seen up until that time.

Several pieces were finished in a rich spinach green with silver threading. The best of them, a tall vase measuring about nine inches in height, was coated with a glossy, mottled, deep brown flambé with orange highlights.

It is not an exaggeration to say that even the simplest piece of Grand Feu, as long as it is marked with the die-stamped "Grand Feu Pottery" designation, will be of superior quality. This is far less true of pieces that are marked "Brauckman Art Pottery." These were made later and are almost always inferior in glazing and the heft of the clay body.

Look for larger pieces, either over six inches tall or exceptionally wide, that are glazed in brighter tones or multi-glazed flambés. Anything with handles, a lid, or reticulated designs should be considered extraordinary. Grand Feu, as stated above, is particularly dense and these pieces are usually undamaged. Those with post-manufacturing flaws will retain most of their value if the damage is limited.

A selection of Grand Feu vases found at a central California estate sale. Even the smallest of these is perfectly fired and perfectly finished.

Grueby Pottery

AMONG POTTERIES EMPLOYING A MORE FORMAL APPROACH
TO CERAMIC DESIGN (as opposed to the Ohr Pottery), Boston's
Grueby Pottery has been the darling of art pottery collectors since
the revival of interest in the movement over thirty years ago.
A friend of mine once described Grueby's aesthetic as organic
naturalism, and I like to say that a good piece of their work
looks more harvested than potted.

Glazing

Grueby Pottery deserved the acclaim for several reasons. First,
their matte glazes were the finest produced in America, inspiring
over one hundred imitators nationwide, from Rookwood to Van
Briggle. While there were numerous companies that were successful in producing rich matte glazes, not one of them consistently
approached Grueby's level of achievement.

William Grueby attempted to replicate the finishes found nat-
urally on gourds and garden
vegetables. The best of his
glazes are rich and even, rather
than drippy, and show a matte,

Date Made: *1905*
Dimension: *9" tall*
Value: *$6,500–8,500*

*While experts will continue to
argue about what constitutes
Grueby's best matte green finish,
this one gets my vote. It is a rich,
deep cucumber matte finish with
intense microcrystalline detailing.*

Date Made: *ca 1900*

Dimension: *15" tall*

Value: *$75,000–100,000*

One of Grueby's rarest and most important forms, decorated with rows of leaves in very high relief. Perhaps only two of these vases exist. From the Zuckerman Collection.

crystalline texture and a nuance of depth. I often use the term *cucumbering* to describe the perfect Grueby finish. This is probably better translated in a photo than verbally, and I've supplied a few close-ups here to show what I mean.

The most common Grueby color is green, and perhaps as much as 90 percent of their hollowware (as opposed to tiles) was covered with it. You would think that, because green is the most readily available, it would be less desirable to collectors than rarer colors such as cobalt blue or ochre. This has never been the case, though some "off color" examples aren't exactly inexpensive.

Date Made: *ca 1900*
Dimension: *10" tall*
Value: *$3,500–4,500*

This might just be a lucky firing flaw, but this rare texture also ranks among the firm's better offerings.

Date Made: *ca 1905*
Dimension: *5" tall*
Value: *$5,000–7,000*

Grueby's "off," or non-green, mattes usually lack the surface nuance shown by the green glazes. The rich, veined texture of this light blue vase is an exception.

Date Made: *ca 1905*
Dimension: *23" tall*
Value: *$13,000–17,000*

A poorly fired matte green piece with tremendous presence. One must be open to the serendipitous effects of kiln-fired glazes. While some buyers avoid pieces such as these, I suggest that the best of them offer some of the best deals available to high-end collectors.

Date Made: *ca 1905*
Dimension: *11" tall*
Value: *$3,000–4,000*

While still a good piece of Grueby ware, the lighter color and relatively flat surface make for an uninspired example of this form. By flat, I mean that there is little nuance to the surface of the glaze and little depth that brings your eye beneath that surface.

In truth, it seems like the success of the glazing is better in green than in any other color. Their matte white, for example, is an excellent glaze, with a rich, oatmeal-like quality and texture. But even the best of white glazes offer a minimum of complexity, with the intricacy of the glazing restricted to the very surface of the pot. Compared with a good matte green, there is little of the visual play that marks white glaze as world class.

The color that comes closest to the quality of Grueby's green matte is yellow, also known as ochre. Perhaps this is because, unlike their light blue or cobalt, it's more consistent with natural hues. But even the ochre lacks the depth of their most popular shade.

It is worth mentioning that Grueby produced more than a single shade of green glaze, and that even the exact coloration varied based on the mix, the pot's placement in the kiln, and how the glaze interacted chemically with the composition of the clay on a given day. The best of these greens were the darker ones, again not only because of the accuracy of the color but because the rich, overall quality was more consistent.

Unless you're amassing a large collection, and your intention is to show the breadth of Grueby's production, I would encourage you to focus on darker green mattes that are evenly fired and possess the subtle cucumbering shown in the photos here. If you're working on a budget, or are interested in collecting a non-mainstream assemblage, look for pieces in ochre, walnut, and light blue.

Multicolored Grueby

Some of Grueby's best work is decorated in more than one color. By this, I don't mean pieces bearing a flambé of different mattes, but rather pots with floral decoration where the blossoms are painted in contrasting hues. These blossoms are most often yellow, but, in ascending order of rarity, might be white, red, or blue. They are usually against a solid background, which is nearly always matte green, but, in ascending order of rarity, can be found in yellow and light blue.

I am not oversimplifying by describing Grueby's work as matte-painted ware, with the decoration covered in rich, non-gloss, kiln-fired glazes. These finishes flowed downward during firing until they cooled. Because of this, they often ran in a way that was not always in the best interest of the final product.

Date Made: *1905*
Dimension: *8" tall*
Value: *$25,000–35,000*

This piece is special in several ways. First, the form and decoration are extremely rare. Second, most multicolored pieces show green grounds with yellow flowers. Green with blue flowers is a most unusual combination. Third, most multicolored pots have simple floral designs. This five-petaled flower is rare. And finally, the crispness of the tooling is accented by the perfect firing of the matte blue.

I've often wondered how much the company anticipated this firing imperfection. In retrospect, it is very clear that the majority of multicolored pieces fired less than perfectly. My guess is that, because a multicolored piece showing no color run is extremely rare, the company did not disregard "drippy" examples to the extent that contemporary collectors do. From my experience, multicolor floral pieces were severely misfired about 50 percent of the time, misfired to an acceptable degree about 20 to 30 percent of the time, fired nearly perfectly about 10 to 15 percent of the time, and perfectly, less than 10 percent of the time.

Date Made: *ca 1905*
Dimension: *5" tall*
Value: *$60,000–70,000*

Another memorable piece of Grueby. The background green is richly textured. The complicated water lily blossom is crisply articulated and the yellow glaze is perfectly fired. Finally, the light green matte in the leaves is unusually textured and fired within the borders of the design.

What the Best Looks Like

Perfectly fired multicolored pieces are probably the worst place for new collectors to start. These are so rare and in such demand that you're almost certain to compete with the most advanced collectors whenever these come to market. Of course, if you can afford it, and have the patience to wait these out, go for it.

I suggest looking for the 30 to 40 percent of the pieces that are mostly successful in their firing, avoiding (unless at bargain rates) the poorly fired 50 percent and the best fired 10 percent. On the right are some examples of Grueby's multicolored pots, showing varying degrees of firing success.

Date Made: *ca 1905*
Dimension: *11" tall*
Value: *$3,000–4,000*

A poorly fired piece of Grueby pottery.

Date Made: *ca 1905*
Dimension: *5" tall*
Value: *$60,000–80,000*

Date Made: *ca 1905*
Dimension: *8" tall*
Value: *$20,000–25,000*

Two more finely decorated pots. The smaller of the two has stylized crocus blossoms on a light blue ground. The taller vase, perhaps unique, shows crisply tooled and perfectly fired lily of the valley with white blossoms and green stems on a blue ground.

Date Made: *ca 1905*
Dimension: *11" tall*
Value: *$10,000–15,000*

Though poorly fired, this is still a respectable piece of Grueby, fired in matte green with a different colored narcissus blossom on three sides. But note how the active background glazing ran to cover the tops of each flower.

Date Made: *ca 1900*
Dimension: *13" tall*
Value: *$45,000–55,000*

One of Grueby's rarest and most impressive forms, this large bulbous vase has rows of flat leaves interspersed with tiny buds under an intensely textured matte green finish.

Grueby patterns often repeat three times around the circumference of the pot. Pieces where the firing is good on two of these three seems like a calculated risk. Bear in mind that these pieces aren't getting any more common as more collectors enter the market every year. I would bet that, just as seasoned furniture collectors have begun to buy pieces by makers other than Gustav Stickley, or better Gustav pieces with some condition issues, pottery collectors are sure to follow suit in the years to come.

If you want a collection where everything is in perfect condition, you're not going to have much of a collection.

Grueby Forms

Grueby pots are always wheel-thrown, unforced (easy-to-pot) forms made of a fairly dense and heavy earthenware base. There are not as many totally different shapes as a new collector might fear. However, since these were individually potted, each marking the artist and the period it was created, there are endless variations of the same form.

It would be impossible to calculate exactly how many totally different shapes were made, but I would guess that the number is fewer than two hundred. Of these, you're not likely to see more than about one hundred over the course of your collecting career. Many of these are not particularly interesting or compelling, and sorting out what is worthy of your collection is actually a lot easier than you might think.

I don't believe a pot has to be large to be fine or great. One of the most memorable pieces of Grueby I've seen was small, green, and minimally decorated. It had a presence, derived from perfect proportions, exemplary glazing, and a light decorative hand. It is true that larger pieces were more time consuming to produce, tended to get more attention during production, and cost more. It is also true that larger pieces tend to be the most impressive on the market today, and are responsible for most of the record prices paid for Grueby's work. Any serious collection should have a large piece or two, if only as an expression of that particular statement. I encourage you only not to become too concerned about size. All things considered, it's overrated.

Date Made: *ca 1900*
Dimension: *11" tall*
Value: *$60,000–80,000*

Another Grueby masterpiece, the handled Kendrick vase has seven rows of leaves and seven applied curving handles. Only a handful of these were glazed in a hue other than matte green.

Date Made: *1900*
Dimension: *18" tall with shade*
Value: *$250,000–300,000*

Arguably the best Grueby ensemble to survive intact, this handled Kendrick is accompanied by its original Tiffany tortoise-shell shade. Note the rich, deep firing of the matte green and the perfectly proportioned shade and base.

More important, regardless of the stature of the pot, are the proportions that are implicit in the product. In these photos, you can see that there are several variations of the same form, each with a different degree of success. The captions, of course, reflect my bias. But my interpretations stem from more than thirty years of developing my eye and listening to the opinions of advanced collectors who understand such nuance well. While proportion is sensed intuitively, I have used a series of photos here to assist you in forming your own opinions.

The last word on Grueby's shape selection centers on the addition of handles or tendrils and leaf channels that further define the form. The least interesting of these are scrolled handles that mimic unrolled fern fronds. These are handsome pieces, also available in a number of varieties, but have a formality to them that limits pricing in spite of their rarity.

Date Made: *1900*
Dimension: *11" tall*
Value: *$20,000–30,000*

A rare reticulated Kendrick vase, this time with a thinner matte green. While this adds some color contrast in that it allows the base clay to show through, the matte green lacks the nuance and depth of a better fired version.

The best of these, variations on the theme created by George Kendrick, have looping handles that curve back to the body of the pot, ending in deep ridges that reach to the base. These examples have a powerful organic quality. The rich glazes that slid down the surface of the pots created a smooth texture in sharp contrast to the roughness of the tooled and scored leaves.

Maker: *T. J. Wheatley Company*
Date Made: *1910*
Dimension: *12¼" tall*
Value: *$3,000–4,000*

This is a period copy by the T. J. Wheatley Company of Cincinnati, Ohio. While a noteworthy attempt, this pot provides some clear reasons Grueby is regarded so highly by contemporary collectors. This is a molded and relatively mass-produced vase, with rounded and flat leaf edges. Further, the proportions of the pot leave it top heavy and ungainly. Finally, the flowing matte green employed by Wheatley is not a bad finish at all, but a pale second when compared with the extraordinary surfaces developed at Grueby.

Tooled Decoration

Beyond form, the decoration that covers a piece of Grueby plays
an integral part in completing the product and further defining
or reinforcing the form. Leaves that trail only halfway up the
sides of a vase are seldom as attractive as those that run from
base to rim. Pots with leaves and no buds usually also are not
as pleasing to the eye. And examples decorated with buds instead
of fully developed blossoms are similarly not as exciting.

My preference here is for maximum coverage, or creative use
of negative space. In other words, the more decoration the better,
unless there is an intelligent, understated use of the parts that
aren't decorated. As with much in this book, such things are
always better shown than stated. I've included additional photos
to illustrate these points below and on the right.

Date Made: *ca 1900*
Dimension: *4" tall*
Value: *$3,000–4,000*

*A perfect cabinet vase, with very sharp edges, total coverage
by the decoration, and an intense dark green matte glaze.*

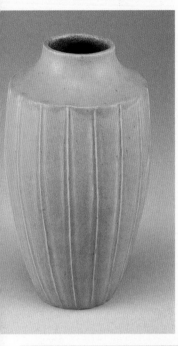

Date Made: *ca 1900*
Dimension: *9" tall*
Value: *$6,000–8,000*

While this is not the richest matte yellow you're likely to find, it still serves as a perfect foil to the highly stylized and subtle leaf decoration on this rare pot.

Date Made: *1900*
Dimension: *7" tall*
Value: *$4,000–5,000*

Another very rare, if simple, form with perfect cucumber matte glazing.

Condition Issues that Lead to Best Buys

MOST OF THE ARTS AND CRAFTS POTTERIES ARE FOR-
GIVEN CERTAIN KINDS OF POST-MANUFACTURING FLAWS.
Grueby, for example, is allowed to have minor nicks and flakes
on the sharply tooled leaf edges that adorn many of their pieces.
The fire is too cool, the earthenware too coarse, and the tooling
too sharp for this very minor malady not to happen over the
course of a century. In fact, if I'm trying to sell a piece of Grueby
to someone who complains about such flakes, they've just
informed me they won't be one of my clients. I feel that such
scrutiny is really just salve for an uncommitted mind.

There are types of damage on grueby pottery that are
very serious and should be avoided in all but the most extreme
circumstances (i.e., the piece is very cheap or very great). Pieces
that have been dropped, shattering into a pile of shards, are
beyond hope. Diametrically opposed long hairlines, the result of
a serious fall, are also a problem that can't be fixed. Such deep
fissures might worsen with age. And, as stated earlier in this
chapter, pieces with severe firing flaws such as murky glazing,
large glaze skips, or serious firing lines across the body will
always be hard to sell.

However, there are a few maladies that seem to have more impact
on pricing and salability than they should, and I suggest these as
instances when you would be more likely to get more Grueby for
your dollar. The most obvious of these, at least to me, are drill
holes through the underside of a Grueby pot. There are several
reasons why these may not be the problem they appear.

First, a good number of grueby's larger vases were
intended as lamp bases, thrown to accommodate oil fonts or,
later, electrical fittings. I have seen far too many pieces of
Grueby with genuine, post-fire, factory drills through the center
of their bottoms that I am certain Grueby did this on a regular
basis. I have even seen factory drills through some or most of the
company markings.

Certainly, there have been a parade of Grueby pieces with drill holes that looked like they were done years after their manufacture by some yahoo with a power drill and too much time on his hands. But even these, unless the entire bottom was removed in the process, can be manageable.

After all, a drill through the center of a pot's bottom won't get any worse, can't be seen when viewing the pot, and perhaps 50 percent of the time, Grueby's workers performed the surgery. Yet, in spite of these facts, drilled pieces lose about 30 to 40 percent of their value and become twice as hard to sell.

Another damage that decreases the cost of quality Grueby pots are base chips. While the majority of the base chips I've seen have resulted from post-manufacturing damage, perhaps 25 percent of them occurred while the piece was being finished at the factory. Often, if fused to the vessel by running glazes, the removal of the stilt (a three-corner ceramic piece used to raise the pot from the kiln floor) caused a tear out of clay and glaze around the foot ring. I've even seen several examples where the factory ground the jagged foot ring smooth, removing most of the chip, and the factory markings, in the process.

In truth, even if a flat base chip occurred after manufacture, it is still the sort of flaw that will not worsen with age and has only a marginal impact on the appearance of the piece. It is worth noting that matte glazes are the easiest for restorers to replicate, so small chips at the base can be rendered nearly invisible.

Nevertheless, pieces with minor stilt pulls or base chips might lose nearly half their value. I encourage you to be more dismissive of such damage on Grueby ware. Once again, as more people become collectors, today's damage will become tomorrow's beauty mark.

Hampshire Pottery

SOME MIGHT QUESTION MY INCLUSION OF HAMPSHIRE POTTERY IN A BOOK devoted to the premium works from the Arts and Crafts period. Purely derivative in the best of cases, work by this company has long been considered a poor man's Grueby. Almost entirely molded, with a repetition of form and design, there is indeed little to recommend. Instead, I suggest focusing on the small part of their work that represents the best of their production.

There is a place, after all, for excellent production pottery from the period that, warts and all, nevertheless captures the look and some of the spirit of the times. Not everyone can afford Grueby and some living above a serious fault line are inclined to hedge their bets.

Hampshire is nearly always molded, and the small percentage of their pieces that are hand thrown are uniformly dreary. These are usually squat pieces with no embossed decoration, bearing thin, green matte finishes. Since we'll be examining only the very best of Hampshire's work, these thrown pieces should be entirely disregarded.

Similar to our earlier evaluation of Grueby pottery, Hampshire pieces are rated by the quality of form and glazing. Size is less a factor here since the repetition of forms makes it clear that their best work tops out at about twelve inches.

Date Made: *ca 1910*
Dimension: *15" tall*
Value: $2,000–3,000

*Fine and large lamp base with original factory fittings.
Like most of the better Hampshire ware, this piece replicates
the leaf-and-bud work of the Grueby pottery.*

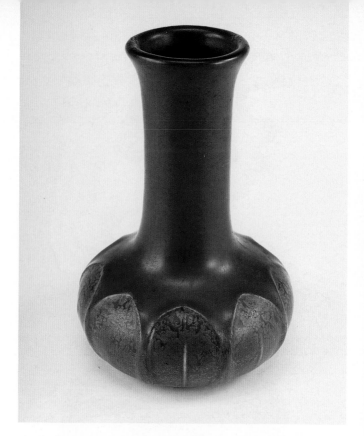

Date Made: *1910*
Dimension: *9" tall*
Value: *$1,000–1,500*

Although a Grueby clone, this pot still has sufficient charm to be of interest. Note the use of secondary glazing to accent the spade-shaped leaves circling the base.

Forms

Larger is still better but most of the interesting Hampshire pieces are usually about eight to ten inches in height and are covered with embossed, spade-shaped leaves in the Grueby style. The term *embossed* means these pieces have decoration that was imparted in the mold. Conversely, designs on Grueby vases were hand tooled and applied to the surfaces of thrown vessels. The more of the surface covered with such decoration, the better. These pieces are simple vessel shapes, swelling towards the top with gently rolled or beaded rims.

There are interesting Hampshire examples with tied bows "gathering" the surface as though it were cloth. Avoid them. You would do well to similarly pass up all but the best undecorated pieces. Instead, look strictly for larger pieces that more closely approximate Grueby's work.

Glazing

Hampshire copied Grueby's work not only in form and decoration but in the quality and colors of glazes they employed. Matte green is probably still the best choice, though Hampshire also applied a rich, flowing, textured matte blue and a rich, pink-purple matte that could also be considered their best offering. In any case, I am inclined to point you towards Hampshire glazes that have some action to them, with thick curdling and the introduction of secondary colors such as cream or yellow.

Date Made: *ca 1910*
Dimension: *9" tall*
Value: *$2,000–3,000*

Large bulbous vase with an excellent feathered blue matte flambé. While at best a molded production pot, it is still a fine piece of American art pottery.

The best Hampshire pieces then are usually under a foot in height, have embossed, stylized leaves, and are covered with rich, textured matte finishes, usually green or blue.

Date Made: *1910*
Dimension: *7" tall*
Value: *$500–750*

Comparing the same form with different glazes, this first vase shows a thin matte green on a Grueby-style form. It's good as far as it goes, but it is a fairly superficial example.

Date Made: *1910*
Dimension: *7" tall*
Value: *$600–800*

With a richer and thicker glaze, this is a better example. Nevertheless, the colors are mostly dark and the pot lacks the contrast needed to make it more interesting.

Date Made: *ca 1910*
Dimension: *7" tall*
Value: *$750–1,000*

The best of the three, with good use of feathered glazing.

Damage

Because Hampshire ware is molded, there are repetitions of form that ultimately have great impact on pricing. A vase with only a small chip will be worth about half as much as a perfect one. Hampshire was nearly always marked in mold and, while a rare, unmarked piece will lose a shade of value, the forms were repeated enough so that factory designations are relatively unimportant.

One last word concerns the later glazed pieces that occasionally surface. My understanding is that a number of Hampshire pieces left the factory in the bisque, unglazed state. There are several stories of how this might have happened, but, ultimately, it's of little concern here. What does matter is that they are now coming to market with glazes that were not imparted by Hampshire, and were probably made by the hands of some "artiste" attempting to pass them off as originals. These are usually bright in color, often glossy, and certainly not Arts and Crafts.

Whatever its origin, Hampshire ware is of interest here only as a lesser Arts and Crafts ware. The high-glazed, colorful pieces have nothing to do with this aesthetic and, in many ways, are not worthy of any serious collection.

Marblehead Pottery

MARBLEHEAD POTTERY IS CONSIDERED ONE OF THE PREMIER PRODUCERS OF ARTS AND CRAFTS WARE. They made their best work from about 1905 until about 1915. We'll evaluate both their decorated and undecorated ware here. Unlike most of the potteries we'll study in this book, Marblehead produced a high level of undecorated work that is certainly worthy of some of the best Arts and Crafts collections.

Undecorated Ware

With the exception of block pieces, such as bookends and decorated wall pockets, and later examples with embossed decorations, such as cream pitchers with Spanish galleons, nearly all Marblehead pottery was hand thrown. The pottery specialized in simple, unforced shapes covered with fine, smooth, or pebble matte finishes. The simplicity of the glazes and shapes, as well as the compatibility of the colors they offered, made for a very satisfying, inexpensive, and handsome product.

In fact, considering that most of their undecorated ware still sells for under $500, there is little from the period that offers as much quality for the money. To be precise, undecorated Marblehead pots offer the perfect low-priced accompaniment to the Arts and Crafts interior.

Date Made: *1915*
Dimension: *4" tall*
Value: *$300–400*

A typical piece of undecorated Marblehead pottery. Even their production ware was hand thrown and covered with one of their fine enamel glazes.

Date Made: *ca 1910*
Dimension: *7" tall*
Value: *$120,000–130,000*

Exceptional ovoid vase with tooled and surface-painted flowers on a green ground. Beautifully executed, well designed, and with sufficient color contrast. This is the piece that set the record for work by this pottery, selling in one of our auctions for $121,000.

Date Made: *ca 1915*
Dimension: *14" tall*
Value: *$2,000–3,000*

A great piece of Marblehead's undecorated ware. The form is large and massive, and the piece is evenly glazed with a fine dark blue matte.

These pieces are usually a single enameled exterior color. The most popular shades are dark green, dark blue, brown, sand, and gray. Less desirable are lavender, light blue, white, light green, and pink. All of these shades are usually accompanied by a contrasting interior color, which normally has no impact on value.

The average undecorated vase is under six inches in height. While the forms are all hand thrown, there are a relatively limited number of shapes. Nearly all Marblehead pieces, regardless of glaze or form, are made of a rich, brick red clay. Marblehead assiduously marked their pieces with their trademark-impressed ship/MP logo.

Damage—even minor chips—will reduce value significantly. While Marblehead are one-of-a-kind pieces, they are far from rare, so collectors will usually wait until a perfect example comes to market.

Look for larger pieces in perfect condition with darker matte finishes in green or blue. Pieces over ten inches in height are extremely rare and will usually sell for over $1,000.

Decorated Ware

There are two kinds of decorated Marblehead, with designs embossed on molded pieces and those imparted strictly by hand. The molded ware is rare and interesting as far as it goes. However, because such pieces are die cast, they are repeatedly found on the market and their value is relatively limited. The most common of these are sailing ship book blocks, parrot and flower wall pockets, and milk pitchers/creamers with Spanish galleons. These are *not* the best of what Marblehead has to offer and should be purchased only when the price is low.

Instead, it would be wiser to consider Marblehead's one-of-a-kind hand-thrown pieces. These are separated into two categories: the first shows designs that are traced onto

Maker: *Hannah Tutt*
Date Made: *ca 1910*
Dimension: *4" tall*
Value: *$20,000–25,000*

Sometimes it is very difficult to explain why one piece is better than another. This is particularly true when assessing Arts and Crafts ware because the design elements are often subtle and the nuances extremely difficult to discern. This pot, for example, is a fairly common form and the decoration is often available in many permutations. However, its color is very unusual, offering excellent contrast with the background, and the tooling is very, very gentle. Note the addition of a second color around the top of the rim.

the thrown surface and then painted in a color, or colors, that offers some contrast to the background. The second, which are far more desirable, are both traced and then modeled or tooled into the surface of the pot. These are better because they add much more clarity to the design. Bear in mind that Marblehead is matte-painted ware with applied colors that often ran in the heat of the kiln. It doesn't take much of an oven fire to blur designs. The gentle modeling almost always offered a crisper result.

Perhaps one in twenty pieces of Marblehead pottery is deco-rated, and perhaps one in thirty is tooled and surface painted. Most decorated Marblehead is under six inches tall. Larger pieces of tooled-and-painted ware represent about 1 percent of the company's output. These represent the most desirable works, and contemporary Arts and Crafts aficionados avidly collect them. As rare as this 1 percent of their production is, the company repeated nearly all their designs to some extent.

Nevertheless, some decorative motifs are rarer still. For example,

Date Made: *ca 1915*
Dimension: *6" tall*
Value: $5,000–6,000

Though larger than most, this dec-orated vase shows a handsome design on a good form. The prob-lem is that the decoration doesn't contrast enough with the back-ground, and the lack of modeling does not ease the lack of clarity.

Date Made: *ca 1910*
Dimension: *6" tall*
Value: *$7,500–10,000*

To illustrate the point, this is essentially the same shape and dec-oration as the last vase but the design is crisply modeled and the background color offers excellent contrast. Expect to pay three times more for this one than the previous one, but you get what you pay for.

Date Made: *pre-1910*
Dimension: *4" tall*
Value: *$5,000–6,000*

An extremely rare and early piece of Marblehead. Pieces from this germinal period, dating prior to 1910, are often heavy and intense with stark geometric decoration. These examples define an important era of this company's work and are eagerly sought by collectors.

Date Made: *ca 1910*
Dimension: *12" diameter*
Value: *$60,000–70,000*

A true masterpiece decorated with stalking panthers. This example has all the elements of Marblehead's best, combining design, definition, modeling, color, and size.

though their stylized grape arbor is a handsome design, it is among the most common Marblehead produced. On the other end of the spectrum is one with lollipop flowers gently modeled into the surface. Perhaps only three of these remain. The last one to hit the auction block realized over $100,000. It was six inches tall.

It is also important to note that many pieces of decorated Marblehead employ only two or three colors, including the background glazing that covers the body of the pot. Further, many decorated pieces have design elements in colors that are so close to the base color of the vase that little contrast is offered. As a rule, the best pieces have at least two or three colors in the decoration, and these colors offer a clear contrast to the background.

Hard-fired Marblehead pieces are usually found in perfect condition. Because of this, as well as the fact that the company often repeated their form and design, a single chip severely reduces the value of most pieces.

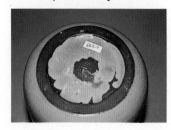

Newcomb College Pottery

IT WOULD BE HARD TO FIND AN ARTS AND CRAFTS PRO-
DUCER WHOSE WARE HAS PROVEN TO BE MORE POPULAR
than that made at Newcomb College. Handmade, individually
crafted and designed, centered in spirit, and evocative of the Old
South, this is art pottery of the highest order. Newcomb College
produced art ware for over forty years, and the vast majority of
it is at least good. As you might suspect, a rather small percentage of their output is extraordinary, and such pieces will be the
focus of this section.

It is an unfortunate reality that, when considering masterpieces in art pottery, we are often forced to consider mostly large
examples by a given company or maker. As I've said before,
taller pieces originally sold for taller sums, and the decorators
knew they had to invest themselves in the piece if they were to
justify the higher material expense. While some of the best
Newcomb ware is, in fact, large, you should take heart in knowing that there are also a num-
ber of smaller pieces that are
equally as captivating.

Each piece of Newcomb
pottery is hand thrown and

Date Made: *ca 1905*
Dimension: *6" tall*
Value: *$7,000–10,000*

*Early Newcomb College vase
with yellow blossoms.*

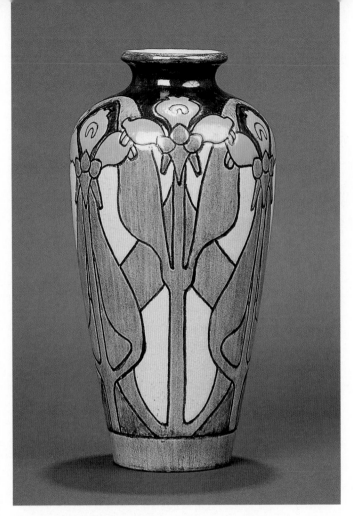

individually conceived, though the quality of design and technique can vary greatly. There were many decorators who passed through the college, mostly students who studied ceramic decoration instead of, or in addition to, the other arts taught there. Only a handful of their decorators were able to consistently create above-average work, and most were the college instructors.

Date Made: *ca 1905*
Dimension: *12" tall*
Value: *$70,000–80,000*

Tall early Newcomb masterpiece with incised and surface-decorated fleur de lis, *the flower of New Orleans.*

For starters, look for pieces executed by Harriett Joor, Henrietta Bailey, Sadie Irvine, Emilie Marie de Hoa LaBlanc, Mary Sheerer, Desiree Roman, Sara Bloom Levy, Leona Fisher Nicholson, and Anna Francis Simpson. I do not mean to exclude all other artists or their work. As always, you must be open to the beauty of the pot, no matter how unexpected. But the most I can hope to do here is assist you in making educated guesses at what pieces are high quality.

Maker: *Henrietta Bailey*
Date Made: *ca 1908*
Dimension: *10" tall*
Value: *$15,000–20,000*

Early vase decorated with incised and surface-painted cherries.

Newcomb's work can be divided into three categories. Their earliest pieces, made from about 1896 until about 1909, were covered in a clear, glossy finish. Pieces from their transitional middle period, from about 1909 until about 1914, were finished in a waxy matte glaze. Most of the Newcomb pottery you'll see on the market is from their last era, from about 1915 until the closing of the pottery in the 1940s. With the exception of some rather dreary glossy pieces made at the very end, all the later Newcomb work has a rich matte glazing.

Early Newcomb Pottery

Pieces of Newcomb ware made prior to 1909 are uncommonly beautiful and compelling. I have also seen some really awful examples, to be sure. But early Newcomb is one of the most consistently qualitative potteries from the Arts and Crafts period.

The average early piece would be a standout at nearly any other company working during the first decade of the century.

With so much to choose from, how do you distinguish the very best from the very good? This is more difficult with Newcomb than with any other American maker except perhaps George Ohr. Newcomb's material is far more literal and accessible than Ohr's, however.

Newcomb ware was either surface painted or both modeled and surface painted. There are some extraordinary pieces to be found without modeling, but 90 percent of the great early Newcomb has at least some carving that sharpen details and adds depth to the designs. Some of the modeling is deeper than on other pieces, and this is usually a plus. But even light tooling can transform a piece into something special.

Date Made: *ca 1905*
Dimension: *9" tall*
Value: *$27,000–32,000*

An early example with nearly the entire surface covered with a tooled floral design. The addition of bold coloring elevates the quality of this piece. This is what great Newcomb pottery should look like.

Maker: *Marie de Hoa LeBlanc*
Date Made: *ca 1903*
Dimension: *8" tall*
Value: *$8,000–12,000*

Very early milk pitcher decorated with cows and trees. While this pot is only surface painted, the naïve rendering of the decoration and the harmony between the decoration and the function of the pitcher are unusual.

Date Made: *ca 1905*
Dimension: *11" tall*
Value: *$12,000–16,000*

Early surface-decorated vase with daffodil.

Color consideration is another important factor in assessing Newcomb ware, especially from this early period. The vast majority of pieces are decorated predominantly in shades of blue, green, and cream. Many times, the designs are outlined in black or a very dark blue. But many of the best pieces show the judicious application of a bright yellow or, more rarely, violet. It is amazing how only a trace of yellow can transform a beautiful example into a masterpiece.

Subject matter is always important, but usually a less critical factor. It is true that collectors will often pay more for an early landscape or a pot decorated with birds or swamp creatures. But repeatedly, many of the most handsome examples of Newcomb ware are decorated with flowers indigenous to the Deep South. I encourage you when considering Newcomb—more than with

Date Made: *ca 1900*
Dimension: *11" diameter*
Value: *$20,000–30,000*

Subject matter isn't always a factor in determining the quality and value of Newcomb ware, but this unique plate showing the campus chapel is an advanced collector's piece.

any other company covered in this book—to trust your eye to determine how beautiful a pot is. One of the things that makes this work so popular is that it is easy to love.

Composition is another critical matter. Most of the best early Newcomb ware is decorated from nearly top to bottom. While it might be acceptable to consider a piece great with less than full coverage, the better ones detail or incorporate at least 85 percent of the exterior surface.

Maker: *Amelie Roman*
Date Made: *ca 1900*
Dimension: *6¼" tall*
Value: *$15,000–20,000*

Another unusual subject. Note how the artist incorporated 80 percent of the surface into the decoration.

Form is another thing we should consider. As a rule, anything other than a tall vase form is usually graded lower. However, Newcomb produced marvelous chocolate pots, graceful low bowls, pitchers, and even cups and saucers. One beautiful piece I saw years ago was an eight-inch-tall jar decorated with sweet pea blossom in blue and cream. The gently modeled design only covered a portion of the surface. Not especially colorful, the

Date Made: *ca 1900*
Dimension: *8" tall*
Value: *$45,000–55,000*

Most Newcomb pieces depict flowers or landscapes. This extraordinary pot shows a continuing band of surface-painted alligators.

Date Made: *ca 1900*
Dimension: *14" tall*
Value: *$75,000–85,000*

Another rarity, this massive, early Newcomb pot is decorated with parading peacocks.

Date Made: *ca 1905*
Dimension: *9" tall*
Value: *$30,000–40,000*

Newcomb fired a few kilns of sang de boeuf high-glaze vases around 1905. Unlike most of these pieces, which fired unevenly, this example shows rich, even coloring.

design only used blue and white. The jar's original lid was intact and decorated both with blossoms and a written line about the flowers. The jar sold for over $40,000. Another covered jar, with yellow blossoms, sold recently at a small auction for over $70,000.

I could give you numerous examples of Newcomb ware that has sold for tens of thousands of dollars. The important thing to remember here is that the overall beauty of the piece, more than the size, subject, or even condition, is what determines the very best.

Date Made: *ca 1905*
Dimension: *7" tall*
Value: *$45,000–55,000*

Early Newcomb sweet pea–covered jar.

The lid to the covered jar with an incised verse.

Date Made: *1905*
Dimension: *12" tall*
Value: *$25,000–35,000*

Early calla lily vase with incised and surface-painted tall calla blossoms. This vase sold in 1997 for over $20,000 in spite of two hairline cracks.

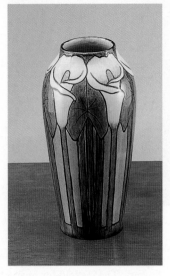

Damage is increasingly acceptable on early high-glazed Newcomb ware. A single rim chip might decrease worth by 10 to 20 percent, but the piece would still be easy to sell. Nearly a decade ago, I sold the twelve-inch vase with two four-inch cracks shown above for over $20,000. If the piece is beautiful and fits the criteria outlined previously, and if the price reflects the condition, buy it.

Transitional Newcomb Pottery

This must have been an odd time to be at Newcomb College because the pottery was changing and modernizing their look. They were moving away from clear, glossy finishes to waxy matte glazing, while ushering in new techniques and decorative styles. While there are some beautiful pieces to be had, most of the transitional ware is seldom better than very good.

It seems that, in searching for a new style, the pottery experimented with changes in composition and color as well. Flowers, for example, seemed to materialize out of the middle of a pot with little or no relation to the overall piece. In contrast to the carving depth achieved in earlier work, transitional pieces often have shallow carving. And the colors tended towards soft and misty greens and blues.

Maker: *Mazie T. Ryan*
Date Made: *1905*
Dimension: *10" tall*
Value: *$10,000–15,000*

Fine transitional Newcomb three-handled loving cup with jasmine blossoms and the motto, "Drink to me only with thine eyes and I will pledge with mine." Note the waxy surface of the glazing, which is neither glossy nor dead matte.

While such experiments were not nearly as good as the work that preceded them, they occasionally led to some interesting innovations. I recall one vase, a pine tree scenic, painted only in tones of medium to dark green and medium blue. The erratic contour of the crowns of the trees defined reticulations, or cutouts, below the top rim of the vase. This was a one in a hundred piece, but it remains one of the better Newcomb landscapes I've encountered from any period.

Maker: *A. F. Simpson*
Date Made: *1910*
Dimension: *9" tall*
Value: *$6,000–8,000*

A well-executed transitional vase. In spite of the subdued color and light carving, the chrysanthemums are well defined.

To ignore Newcomb's work from the transitional period because it is often confused and uneven would be to deprive your collection of potentially exciting pieces. I suggest here that you be very, very particular when buying pieces made during this time. The best will be visually strong in spite of the misty glazing and limited color schemes. Designs should reach from top to bottom, and carving should have some depth (though, it is important to note that transitional pieces are, at best, moderately carved). Condition is always a factor. However, since great transitional pieces are extremely rare, I encourage you to be more forgiving than usual.

Maker: *A. F. Simpson*
Date Made: *ca 1915*
Dimension: *11" tall*
Value: *$18,000–23,000*

A first-rate carved Newcomb matte bayou scene. Notice the depth of cut, the detailing in the moss, and the strong colors. While the addition of a full moon never hurts, it seems that more emphasis is placed on that component than on the overall strength of the pot.

Date Made: *ca 1920*
Dimension: *6" tall*
Value: *$3,000–4,000*

The carving and color of the landscape on the pot to the right are more muted than most.

Date Made: *ca 1910*
Dimension: *8" tall*
Value: *$3,000–4,000*

To the left is a colorful, if blurry, transitional vase.

Late Newcomb Pottery

Most of the Newcomb ware you'll see on the market today will be later work covered with their fine matte glazing. By the time they began producing matte-glazed pottery, the firm had achieved a great deal of acclaim and demand for their work was peaking. Nevertheless, as consistently good as their middle period proved to be, Newcomb's later period was their least interesting. One can only imagine how Sadie Irvine felt carving bayou scene after bayou scene. In truth, you'd be hard pressed to find a bad one, and equally challenged to find an exceptionally fine example.

I have seen a few matte pieces decorated with birds, but about 80 percent of the pieces from this period are florals and the rest are variations of landscapes, mostly bayou scenes. Subject matter

is, again, less important than the visual power of the piece, and handsome scenics far out-number extraordinary florals. There are several factors that contribute to this, revolving mostly around depth of cut, detailing, strength of color, and definition achieved through contrasting colors.

Date Made: *ca 1920*
Dimension: *6" tall*
Value: *$4,000–5,000*

Examples with lids are very rare. Pieces with reticulation are even rarer.

Maker: *A. F. Simpson*

Date Made: *ca 1915*

Dimension: *11" tall*

Value: *$14,000–18,000*

Another excellent bayou scene showing the strong carving usually associated with the best of this genre.

Date Made: *ca 1920*
Dimension: *8" tall*
Value: *$5,000–6,000*

An unusually colorful piece of matte Newcomb ware.

Colors

The majority of matte pieces have blue backgrounds and the decoration is usually rendered in blues, soft greens, and cream or ivory. As a rule, the darker and bolder the blue, the better the piece. In florals, the addition of rich mint greens and soft pinks are always a plus. Landscapes are usually rendered only in tones of blue and light green (though about half of them have a creamy yellow moon). Again, the stronger the blue, the better.

I have seen only a few landscapes with deep purple backgrounds. These are quite rare and are worth buying in nearly any condition. The last one we sold, over a decade ago, brought nearly $4,000, in spite of having two hairline cracks. I have not sold one since, in any size or any condition.

Carving

Since all matte pieces are at least lightly modeled, carving is a critical element in overall quality. For the most part, pieces with shallow carving lack the depth, detail, and intensity of those with deeper modeling. I should point out here that the quality of carving refers not only to the depth between the surface and the background but, perhaps more importantly, the detailing in the surface within the decoration. Great landscapes, for example, have the detailing of muscle-like fibers within the trunks. And florals, at least the best examples, actually allow you to see into the blossom, providing the illusion of depth.

One last point concerns coverage. Most matte Newcomb pieces show decoration on only about half the surface of the pot. The best pieces are usually decorated from top to bottom. This is not unusual on scenic vases, which are nearly always decorated that way. But a floral matte vase with extensive coverage, especially if it is a taller piece, is extremely unusual.

The best pieces are ten inches or taller in height; deeply carved with fine surface detailing, with decoration covering the majority of the pot; and glazed in deep, rich colors.

Subject

While a great scenic will usually bring more than a great floral, the latter are much harder to find. Even within scenic pieces there is an accepted hierarchy. Bayou scenes are the most common, though unusual variations are extremely desirable. Simple permutations are those with light pink backgrounds. The deeper the pink, the better the piece. In addition, some bayou scenes are augmented with carved fences, houses, or rarely, recognizable buildings (like the chapel from Newcomb College). Such decorative embellishments will often double the value of a similar piece without them.

Condition

Minor damage hurts the value of matte Newcomb more than it does the early high-glazed ware. A fingernail chip to the rim might be met with a drop in price of about 40 to 50 percent. But remember this: there is a lot of fine Newcomb decorated ware on the market and most of it dates to after 1915. If you find one that is truly exceptional based on the previous information, be willing to give it the respect and consideration it deserves.

Maker: *Cynthia Littlejohn*
Date Made: *1920*
Dimension: *7" tall*
Value: *$10,000–12,000*

A truly great matte Newcomb vase, this pot is deeply carved, modeled, and painted from top to bottom and colored in green, blue, cream, and yellow.

Ohr Pottery

OHR POTTERY IS PROBABLY THE MOST DIFFICULT ART
POTTERY FOR US TO ASSESS because George Ohr, as well as
the ware he produced, was endlessly creative. This was an artist
who constantly experimented with the very idea of potting, and
you have to get into his head at least a little bit to have any sense
of how good a given vessel might be. After having personally
viewed nearly half of what Ohr produced during his career, it is
clear that the artist went through creative spasms that explored
initially the relationship between glaze and form and, ultimately,
form without glaze.

Much of Ohr's better work describes the process of his experimental nature. As you see more of his work, and there are enough
books and auction catalogs in print that cover perhaps a thousand
examples, you can begin to tie together themes based on the clays
he chose, the manipulative techniques he used, and the glazes he
employed. You can begin to recreate how Ohr worked through
ideas in fixed periods of time, such as how long a glaze batch
lasted before it dried out or he used it up.

There are a series of heavily manipulated, hand-sized bulbous
vases predominantly glazed in a bright red. These all seem to
share secondary glazes of cream, gun metal, and blue. There are
at least seven vases that are so similar in color as to be clearly
related. It is obvious that Ohr decided to pursue this particular
idea to its extreme, thinking it out on the wheel and finally in
the kiln before moving onto his next scheme. As you might
expect, some are better and more successful than others, and
therein lies the rub of assessing Ohr's work.

His totemic pots were another matter. Having viewed about
eight of these over the years, they are uniformly phallic in shape
and covered with stark matte black, gun metal, or black-green
finishes, usually with a light gloss. They are totally different from

Date Made: *ca 1900*
Dimension: *9" tall*
Value: *$70,000–80,000*

Exceptional George Ohr vase with two scrolled handles under a green and mottled red flambé.

the bulk of his work, lacking the characteristic twists and ruffles and vibrant glazing that most collectors cherish. Yet, because of their oddness and unusual size (they average over twelve inches), contemporary collectors avidly seek them out. I mention these here because, while they are nearly the opposite of the series of red, manipulated vases mentioned earlier, they are another example of how Ohr chose to explore and develop themes.

Date Made: *ca 1900*
Dimension: *6" tall*
Value: *$55,000–65,000*

A great oversized, elegant teapot with a serpentine spout and a rich pink-and-orange flambé.

Date Made: *ca 1900*
Dimension: *5" tall*
Value: *$80,000–90,000*

Another great teapot, with a blister pink glaze and an applied snake.

To further complicate matters, Ohr also repeated ideas and forms, such as teapots or manipulated pitchers, throughout his career. Later ones are usually better, with more complicated forms and brighter glazing. It is in reviewing these forms that Ohr favored throughout his career that we can best assess the potter and his craft.

Let's explore this point by taking a closer look at Ohr's teapots. I've seen and handled over fifty of them, including a double pot (half coffee, half tea), cadogans (trick-bottom loaders with fused lids), snake-clad vessels, little ones with stubby handles, schizophrenic examples with one side in blue and the other in a bright red, and so on. While much of his spasmodic work seems restricted to a brief period of time, the teapots are a leitmotif that spanned much of his career. But the teapots with the earlier marks are clearly more traditional in style and glazing, favoring darker tones of green and brown. They look more like something you might actually brew tea in. As his art matured, Ohr worked as though he was less bound by tradition and more enchanted by the abstract. His teapots became elongated and sensual. The glazing was marvelously weird and colorful. And the pots were augmented with applied snakes or in-body manipulations.

This is not to say that all later Ohr is better and all early Ohr is finely made but not terribly interesting. The man was a master, yet there are masterpieces and duds from all periods. But, as a rule, Ohr pieces made after the Biloxi fire of 1893 tend to be more abstract, colorful, and nutty. To simplify the complicated, look for these.

Date Made: *ca 1900*
Dimension: *7" tall*
Value: *$90,000–100,000*

A truly exceptional oversized teapot, with a double-kink handle, serpentine spout, unusual finial, and dynamite glaze.

I could probably fill a book of this size with Ohr's work alone. But, as Ohr himself once said, you can judge his work by looking at ten pieces as well as you can the work of Shakespeare by reading ten lines of a sonnet. Let's accept that the effort that follows excludes much, much more than it covers.

When it concerns Ohr, I encourage you to look deeply before you leap. If you are serious about collecting Ohr, you should begin by purchasing every book published showing his pieces. The *Mad Potter of Biloxi: The Art and Life of George E. Ohr,* by Garth Clark, Eugene Hecht, and Robert Ellison, is a fine place to start. Another book worth the price of admission is *After the Fire, George Ohr: An American Genius,* by Eugene Hecht. Finally, you can get a sense of contemporary pricing by checking out previ-

Date Made: *ca 1900*
Dimension: *3 ½" tall*
Value: *$10,000–15,000*

A fine, hand-sized, open-mouthed, manipulated red vase. While only three-and-a-half inches tall, this piece packs a lot of punch for its size.

ous auction catalogs at www.ragoarts.com, where hundreds of pieces are pictured and priced.

Forms

One of the underlying themes of this book is keep it simple and, to that end, I will be very direct in instructing you about what to look for. You can find any number of interesting, if modest, pieces at any given time. These are usually smallish (under four inches) examples with dark glazes (variations and flambés of brown, green, black, or a combination of these), with little to no manipulation. As interesting as these might be, they are far from Ohr's best work and are not his primary focus.

Date Made: *ca 1900*
Dimension: *10" tall*
Value: *$25,000–35,000*

A tall and exceptional piece of Ohr, with a manipulation restricted to the top, and the body finished with a brilliant and unusual red and green flambé.

Much of Ohr's form selection (excluding trick pieces, teapots, and some really weird ones that are probably of alien origin) can more or less be categorized in one of four ways. Forms include manipulated pieces that retain the pot form, manipulated pieces that are free form, straight-sided pieces with a small percentage of manipulation at the top or bottom, and straight-sided pieces with no manipulation. I list these not because I suggest that one is better than any other, but merely to assist you in identifying and describing Ohr's work on your own.

Ohr tended to work best in hand-sized pieces, those under six inches tall that he could manipulate easily and where the various elements could be integrated into a single pot. I have seen a number of tall masterpieces, to be sure. But much of the great Ohr is under seven inches in height. The difficult part is deciding which combination of form, glazing, and concept work best. Look for shapes that have a completeness to them, where, regardless of size, the form and manipulation are compelling.

Let's move on to these other elements in order to get a fuller picture.

Glazes

As mentioned earlier, most of Ohr's pots were covered in variations of black and green, often not to their advantage. I am not of the belief that a piece has to be brightly colored to be special, though clearly much of his best glazed work is extremely colorful. But there are, for example, variations of gun-metal black with silver threading and matte crystals that rank among Ohr's best glazes. Nevertheless, since most of Ohr's work tended to be glazed in darker colors, and since many of his more scintillating finishes are bright glazes or combinations of glazes, most of his more expensive pots are brilliant in color. Look for red, orange, pink, emerald green, sky blue, and white. Multiple glazes are almost better than single glazes. Also, in keeping in form with Ohr's quirkiness, some of his most interesting pieces use different glazes on different sides.

Date Made: *ca 1900*
Dimension: *4" tall*
Value: *$8,000–12,000*

One of Ohr's schizophrenic glazing examples, with each of two sides in totally different finishes.

Another consideration is texture. Ohr played with the surface of his glazes almost as much as he toyed with color. While most of his finishes were clear and glossy, some are a densely veined matte and others have a coarse, blistered feel to them. Ohr also at times mixed color and varying surface textures.

Date Made: *ca 1900*
Dimension: *11" tall*
Value: $80,000–90,000

Tall goose-necked pitcher with a brilliant pink and black-and-white flambé. While there is no in-body manipulation, the elegant form is reinforced by the curving handle and pulled spout. Another example of how Ohr's work is often about so much more than manipulation of surface.

Manipulation

I have seen pieces distressed to within an inch of their lives. They can be far less interesting than others with a single in-body twist. Usually, the more handwork, the better, but Ohr's pieces are best described when considering the totality of the piece. In-body twists are usually more interesting because, though manipulated, they retain the original form. Look for pieces with asymmetrical handwork, where the stress on one side is different from the manipulation on the other. Extreme decoration, such as pieces with holes punched through the body, torn rims, or deeply dented sides are often very good.

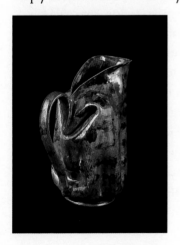

Date Made: *ca 1900*
Dimension: *10" tall*
Value: *$85,000–95,000*

Another great pitcher, with a blinding red-and-black flambé. Note how one side of the piece is heavily folded, while the other is smooth and even.

Date Made: *ca 1905*
Dimension: *5" tall*
Value: *$8,000–10,000*

A great scroddled Ohr bisque with an asymmetric form and blended clays.

Bisque Ware

We used to think that Ohr's unglazed pieces, those only bisque-fired with no finishing glazes, were incomplete. You could buy the best of them in the 1970s for about $50 each. Some fool even glazed a few hundred of them with lifeless, plastic-like finishes, mostly in red, and managed to trick most of us for a week or two. We were all to discover later that Ohr's bisque ware, those pieces made mostly after about 1902, were his most complete work. As Ohr himself said, "God put no color in souls, and I'll put no color on my pots." There was probably no purer expression of the Arts and Crafts in American decorative arts as there was in Ohr's bisque-fired ware. His work has immediacy, creativity, and surreal beauty.

Date Made: *ca 1905*
Dimension: *9" tall*
Value: *$20,000–25,000*

While not scroddled, this tall bisque vase is heavily
manipulated, incised, tooled, and inscribed.

Just as Gustav Stickley chose the intense grain of quartersawn American oak as decoration, Ohr often mixed clays to form a swirling "scroddled" effect. What need was there for decoration when the materials themselves provided color and pattern?

Further, his later work was far more abstract than anything that preceded it. Forget, for a moment, that such pieces could never be used as vases because they would leech water. More important was the manipulation of the form to such an extreme that any utilitarian purpose was impossible to determine. This

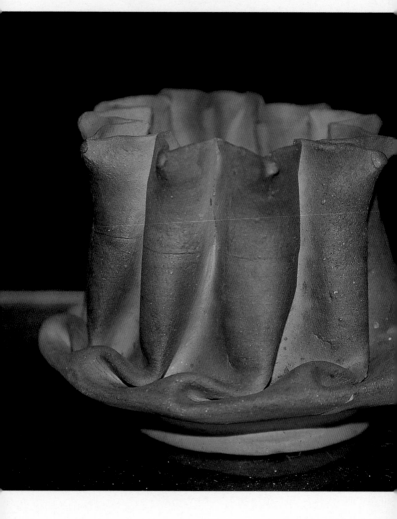

late work, which was initially dismissed by the Arts and Crafts community at large, is probably Ohr's single most important contribution to period decorative arts.

Look for scroddled pieces with severe and unrelenting manipulation. Certainly, if you see a bisque piece of a single clay with the same level of distress, that piece is more important than a simple blended one. I have also seen single clay pieces with writing (poems, dedications, etc.), applied handles and/or snakes, and tooled decoration. These are rare and quite good.

Date Made: *ca 1905*
Dimension: *5" tall*
Value: *$7,500–8,500*

A lovely pleated vase. While only made of red clay, minerals in the mix were brought to the surface in the firing, achieving a metallic sheen as a second color.

Condition

Each thrown Ohr piece is one of a kind. He bragged about that, and it was nearly always true. (The exceptions are many of his puzzle mugs, and most of the fair trinkets he produced to help pay the bills.) That said, if you like a piece and the idea it represents, you'll have to love it as you find it or you'll have to forget about it.

There are several practical reasons that Ohr's work often has at least some sort of post-manufacturing flaw. First, these pieces were nearly all stored unwrapped in the attic of his pottery building for decades. They are low-fired, paper-thin, and very fragile. When they were moved from time to time, there was always some damage inflicted upon some of them even by the most careful of hands. And I know of perhaps two hundred pieces that have been damaged, from minor chips to total losses, since Ohr's rediscovery thirty-five years ago.

Damage reduces value on Ohr's work less than any other American pottery. In fact, were you to find a truly great piece with relatively minor damage (minor rim chip repairs, short tight lines, etc.), it would probably not reduce the piece's value by more than 10 percent. In addition, such pieces would be nearly as easy to sell with minor damage as they would if they were perfect.

Bisque pieces, because of their extremely fragile nature, nearly always have some minor nicking to edges. Similarly, minor damage on these pieces has nearly no negative impact on pricing.

Reproductions

A word of caution: it remains an irony that our most inimitable potter is the one most dogged by fakes and frauds. Most of the Ohr fakes come in two varieties. Early on, when we still believed there was something unfinished about the bisque ware, a couple of boneheads from New Jersey took to glazing them with contemporary finishes of their own creation. While they were able to sell these to an unsuspecting public for a time, they ultimately ruined hundreds of authentic vases by augmenting them with terrible, thick, and lifeless glazing.

These are usually (but not always) marked with Ohr's later, incised GEOhr script signature, since most of the bisque work was done during his last period. The bottoms are bereft of nearly any manufacturing blemishes such as long stilt pulls or sloppy glazing. And the glazes reflect light like plastic rather than glass. Once you see a few of these, it is not difficult to tell them from the genuine articles.

A more insidious fake, which also seems to have come from my own Garden State, are total fakes, from the ground up. These are nearly always made of a soft pink clay, rolled rather than thrown, and raised up the side of a tumbler or raised with thick fingers. The manipulations are usually restricted to ruffled rims, and these are nearly always covered with black metallic glazes. They are die-stamped, using printer's letters, with a mark similar to Ohr's. While they might fool the casual observer, they are minor pots in the best of cases.

When in doubt about a piece of Ohr, send a photo of the piece including a shot of the bottom to info@ragoarts.com for a free opinion.

Pewabic Pottery

THERE ARE TWO TYPES OF PEWABIC THAT ARE WORTHY OF MAJOR ARTS AND CRAFTS COLLECTIONS, each totally different from the other. The first, their hand-tooled early ware, was produced for a short time and is extremely rare. The second, famous for its rich, iridescent flambés, was made for decades.

Date Made: *ca 1905*
Dimension: *13" tall*
Value: *$8,000–12,000*

A fine and early piece of modeled Pewabic pottery with an organic, tooled shoulder.

Date Made: *ca 1915*
Dimension: *11" tall*
Value: *$3,000–5,000*

Most Pewabic ware is covered in blue iridized glazes. Their best work may include blue glazing, but look for multi-glazed flambés with textured surfaces, such as on this handsome pot.

Date Made: *ca 1905*
Dimension: *10" tall*
Value: *$8,000–12,000*

*Another rare, early piece of modeled
Pewabic. These matte pieces were
produced for only a few years, and
perhaps only fifty of them still exist.
This is one of the better examples.*

Early Work

When Pewabic first began producing pots, around 1905, Mary
Chase Perry was responsible for most of the work. Perry designed
a fairly small offering of hollowware that was hand thrown or
built. She usually decorated pieces with modeled blossoms
and/or leaves. She frequently covered these with rich matte
green finishes, though I have also seen flowing browns and
a slate gray.

The best of these are usually nine inches or taller, deeply
modeled, and covered with flowing matte green glazes.
Because they are unique, and were produced for less than
five years, you should consider buying this work with anything less than extensive dam-
age. They are that important
and that rare.

Date Made: *ca 1905*
Dimension: *7" tall*
Value: *$2,000–4,000*

*A most unusual and early example,
this piece is rare because of the
eggplant form and the matte
aubergine finish. This may be the
only lidded piece from this period.*

These early pieces are marked differently from the later work. They are marked with either the die-stamped word *Pewabic* alone, or in conjunction with an arc of oak leaves. It is not uncommon to find these early pieces unmarked, or with marks hidden by the thick glazing that often covered the bottom.

Iridescent Work

Pewabic produced iridescent glazed pottery for decades. While the earlier work is marked somewhat differently than later examples, it is important to remember that some of the more exciting of these have later marks. Trust your eye more than your mind on this ware.

Date Made: *ca 1910*
Dimension: *10" tall*
Value: *$4,000–6,000*

An exceptional early two-handled pot with a rich flambé of two contrasting matte glazes. While their best work from this period is usually accompanied by modeled decoration, advanced collectors are open to extraordinary pieces such as this.

Date Made: *ca 1915*
Dimension: *8" tall*
Value: *$1,000–2,000*

While some of the best pieces of Pewabic are glazed in blue, odd colors such as this gold iridescent finish are among the most prized. The metallic gray secondary glaze makes this a superior example.

Date Made: *ca 1915*
Dimension: *9" tall*
Value: *$1,500–2,500*

Even more common blue glazes are improved by contrasting colors or textures. The semi-volcanic finish on this pot makes for an especially fine example.

The best pieces, as usual, tend to be larger and powerful. I have seen some extraordinary miniatures, as well as handsome examples in all sizes. But larger is definitely better here, and the artists that glazed mammoth pieces normally lavished more attention on them.

Most iridescent Pewabic comes in single shades of blue or green. I would suggest not only looking for more vibrant colors, such as gold or red, but focusing on pieces with a combination of these finishes. Also, I prefer those that have more than a patchwork of glazing, such as pieces with contrasting drips drawn down the side during firing.

Better are pieces with thick, lumpy coats. I recall one piece, mostly in shades of orange, that looked as though crayons had been blowtorched onto the side of the pot. It was, for the record, a later example. It is still one of the best such pieces I've seen, against a backdrop of more than one thousand Pewabic vases.

The mark used almost exclusively on these is a die-stamped circle with the words *Pewabic Detroit* around the circumference. Later marks are identical except the letters *PP* are in the middle of the circle.

Buyers are more discerning when it comes to paying for Pewabic with damage. But, as always, the better the piece, the less damage seems to hinder price or salability.

Date Made: *ca 1915*
Dimension: *9" tall*
Value: *$1,000–2,000*

Another beautiful pot with a blue iridescent foundation, this time augmented with a flambé of two additional colors.

The firm's die-stamped circular mark.

Redlands Pottery

THE AMOUNT OF INTEREST AND MONEY AMERICAN ARTS
AND CRAFTS COLLECTORS have lavished on Redlands Pottery
often defies understanding. Redlands was a small company that
lasted for a brief period of time in the wilderness of Redlands,
California, producing a limited number of molded, low-fire, red
clay pieces, usually embossed with critters or insects. While these
examples all seem to have benefited from a second firing, many
are finished in either a simple red clay color or embellished with
a burnished, bronze-like patina.

Date Made: *ca 1905*
Dimension: *4" tall*
Value: *$25,000–35,000*

*As far as the market is concerned, this is the best Redlands pot yet to have
sold, realizing $31,000 at one of our Craftsman auctions. Nevertheless,
the quality and overall feel of this piece is no better or worse than any
other piece the firm produced.*

Date Made: *ca 1905*
Dimension: *2" tall*
Value: *$16,000–20,000*

This crab vase, made of the same soft red clay employed by the firm, was produced in two sizes. This is the smaller of the two versions.

So what's the attraction? It would be facile to suggest that the relative scarcity is the single reason for pricing. There are other considerations as well.

We auctioned a tapering vase with embossed sharks, with minor scuffing to the low-fire surface, for over $30,000. The phone lines at that sale were filled with buyers from across the country, including some of the most astute collectors the field has ever known.

I can suggest that the form of that particular pot was strong, a small volcano of a piece, completely covered with swirling sharks in bold relief. The finish, though slightly marred with wear, was both soft and quietly powerful in a fashion simply not seen from this period. It was the only known example of the form, and the piece was new to the market, having surfaced from a new source in the California desert.

But to understand the disproportionate interest in the piece is to understand Redlands specifically and Arts and Crafts decorative ceramics in general. There was an overall fineness to the piece manifest both in the design and the quality. It possessed a quietude that said much about prewar California, a sensitivity towards the environment it depicted and the rich natural clays it contained. I'm trying here to describe spirit and, like many before me, I've probably failed. This pot, like the rest of Redlands' production, is better felt than described.

Date Made: *ca 1905*
Dimension: *3" tall*
Value: *$13,000–17,000*

About five of these pieces have been found over the last thirty years. They remain a favorite among art pottery collectors. Notice the burnished metallic quality to the finish.

Date Made: *ca 1905*
Dimension: *4" tall*
Value: *$13,000–17,000*

*This covered pot is the companion
piece to a volcano-shaped
shark vase.*

I've spent time here outlining the best of the best of Redlands. It is important to note that even lesser pieces sell for upwards of $10,000 each when in reasonably original condition. I suggest here that any piece of Redlands ware with embossed decoration (because, once again, it is entirely molded) is worthy of your collection.

The pieces that have so far surfaced are decorated with embossed designs about 90 percent of the time. Popular motifs are almost entirely animated creatures, including frogs, sharks, and spiders. There are also pieces with eucalyptus leaves and pods. The best of these have a fine, burnished bronze patina, mostly free of scuffing. Nearly all pieces are under six inches in height.

Pieces are always marked with an embossed tadpole in a circle. Because of the low-fire nature of the ware, these often have scuffed surfaces and minor nicking to the top rim. Minor damage will reduce value by about 15 percent.

*The company's embossed
tadpole mark.*

Roblin Pottery

I HAVE A RESPECT FOR ROBLIN WARE THAT IS NOT DIS-
SIMILAR TO THE ESTEEM in which I hold Redlands Pottery.
I am similarly baffled by the appeal it continues to hold for me.
I had the privilege long ago to see and handle part of the Dora
Robertson estate, which included 90 percent of what remained
of Roblin pottery. While in operation in San Francisco for nearly
a decade, the majority of what Roblin produced was destroyed
in the San Francisco earthquake of 1906.

Beyond this sobering statistic is the fact that most of what
remains is small, undecorated and, in many cases, unglazed. Add
to the mix Alexander Robertson's extremely limited shape selection, much of which is simple, footed cylinders. In the Roblin
vernacular, a beaded midsection counts as extreme decoration.

Two typical pieces of Roblin. This is such understated ware that it usually escapes the interest of most pottery collectors. Nevertheless, it remains in its simplicity one of this country's finest art potteries.

An exceptional two-handled, unusually large Roblin vase with a polychrome flambé and great glaze. Made of the country's finest red clay.

Maybe the appeal is, as with Redlands, the simplicity and quietude the pieces reflect of the Golden State prior to the land rush that was to follow during the Depression several decades later. When American ceramic artists migrated west at the turn of the century (in the Robertsons' case from Massachusetts), they found an unspoiled wonderland with lush vegetation, wild animals, extraordinary natural clays, and glorious sunsets. I believe the best of the California potteries capture this era, preserving it in three-dimensional form.

Maker: *Linna Irelan*
Date Made: *ca 1905*
Dimension: *5" tall*
Value: *$2,500–3,500*

A finely decorated piece from Scott Goldstein's collection.

Roblin is separated into two distinct categories, decorated and undecorated. We can get picky here and suggest a third designation, separating beaded pieces from plain ones. But let's not. Most of what you'll see, and there won't be much, will be pieces without tooled and/or slip-painted designs. There is precious little available on the open market that shows even a single brush stroke of a blossom.

Date Made: *ca 1905*
Dimension: *4" tall*
Value: *$300–500*

This is a noteworthy Roblin vase in that it is poorly glazed and misfired. Alexander Robertson seemed to have exercised a great deal of quality control over his small firm's output.

Decorated Ware

Ninety-nine percent of all Roblin is small in size, under five inches in height. I have seen a series of decorated plates measuring about seven inches in diameter. You can consider these immense. But the best of their decorated vessels are about four inches tall, perfectly thrown, of the finest clays, often with bisque finishes, and painted by Linna Irelan with blossoms in a precise slip relief, occasionally augmented with light modeling.

One such piece might be described as having a bulbous body with a flaring rim and a flaring base made of buff, bisque-fired clay, with a spray of white clover in slip relief. Within this aesthetic, this is a masterpiece, and one that fits in the palm of your hand at under four inches tall.

More ambitious, and less successful, are a small series of luncheon plates with scenes of the Arabian desert or a frog pond, both in slip relief and/or with gentle incising. It is worth noting that the hammering technique that the Robertsons used while at the Chelsea Keramic Art Works in Chelsea, Massachusetts, was used on one of these, evenly applying dents into the soft clay surface.

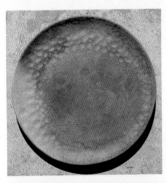

Maker: *Linna Irelan*
Date Made: *ca 1905*
Dimension: *7" diameter*
Value: *$1,500–2,500*

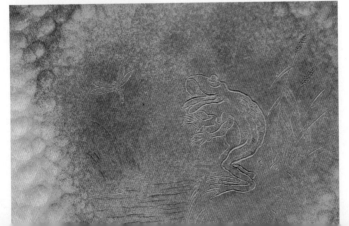

Maker: *Linna Irelan*
Date Made: *ca 1905*
Dimension: *3¼" tall*
Value: *$2,200–2,800 (if in perfect condition)*

Unusual modeled Roblin vase with tooled and applied mushrooms on a white bisque-fired body. One of the only modeled pieces of Roblin still in existence.

In addition, and still rarer, are pieces with tooled and applied decoration. One of the few such examples shows modeled mushrooms adhered to the surface of a four-inch-tall vase of white clay. The vase was bisque fired. It is missing decoration and has minor damage, yet it is still worth over $1,000.

Undecorated Ware

Even though nearly all Roblin ware is undecorated, even plain pieces are extremely rare. As mentioned earlier, there are undecorated examples, and *really* undecorated pieces to be found. The typical Roblin piece is buff, red, white, or medium brown and about four inches tall. Aside from simply thrown forms, Roblin usually has no glazing or decoration of any kind.

The next step up is a slightly larger form, just under four inches tall, a bit more complicated than a simple cylindrical body. There is no glazing on these either but there are one or more "beaded" designs in the body or at the top/bottom rim.

The best of these is exactly like the example on the previous page except there is an evenly applied glazing. These are usually gloss finishes, sometimes clear but usually colored. Rarer are matte finishes, which are next to impossible to find. The best glazed Roblin, and I think I've only seen one or two such examples, are pieces with a dappled polychrome finish.

Roblin is usually marked with one of several die-stamped designations, including a bear (in honor of California) or, in block letters, *Roblin*. Perhaps because most of the surviving Roblin pieces stayed in the family since 1906, the vast majority of pieces are in perfect condition. Pieces with slip or incised designs are worth buying in nearly any condition. Minor damage will knock about 20 percent off the value of such pieces.

Die-stamped Roblin mark.

Rookwood Pottery

I ALMOST EXCLUDED ROOKWOOD FROM THIS BOOK
because the jury is still out as to whether they actually made Arts
and Crafts pottery or just produced a limited body of work that
reflected the style of the period. Ultimately, even though they
may not have been aligned spiritually with the Arts and Crafts
movement, they made some mighty attractive pots and developed some very interesting decorative styles and techniques.
Rookwood was one of America's most consistently qualitative
producers and, for that reason alone, deserves inclusion here.

Rookwood worked in a number of styles over many years,
including Victorian, Art Nouveau, Impressionism, and Moderne.
Their Arts and Crafts–oriented decorative ware was made mostly from about 1900 to 1910. All of their better Arts and Crafts

Maker: *Kataro Shirayamadani*
Date Made: *ca 1901*
Dimension: *12" tall*
Value: *$35,000–45,000*

*Exceptional Rookwood iris glazed pot with geese in flight over a softly
lit marsh. This example is included here not because it is a typical
example of the company's Arts and Crafts ware, but because it was
made during the time the firm was exploring a host of new decorative
styles. Unfortunately, little of their Arts and Crafts work approaches
the level of their best Art Nouveau examples in visual strength or
mastery of technique. From the Zuckerman Collection.*

Maker: *Kataro Shirayamadani*
Date Made: *ca 1901*
Dimension: *11" tall*
Value: *$18,000–22,000*

*This pot is among the best work Rookwood executed in the
Arts and Crafts style. While the pot itself is molded, the tulips
are carved in heavy relief. The bronze appliqué is another
sophisticated touch pioneered in America by Rookwood.*

Maker: *Albert Valentien*
Date Made: *ca 1905*
Dimension: *10" tall*
Value: *$8,000–12,000*

Unusual modeled matte vase with an embossed mermaid. The wave-like modeling to the molded pot, the decorative motifs, and the glazing are all mutually reinforcing. One of the better matte figurals produced by Rookwood.

lines, including painted, modeled, and carved mattes, relied exclusively on molded, rather than hand-thrown, blanks.

Perhaps their most curious contributions are a series of molded and hand-sharpened figural vases in the style of Artus Van Briggle's work in Colorado Springs. While one might convincingly argue that such pieces were Art Nouveau in style, I maintain that this belongs to the ongoing debate about whether the Arts and Crafts in America was really an extension of Art Nouveau. How would one classify Van Briggle's *Lorelai* vase if not as both?

There are several factors that make Rookwood's work less Arts and Crafts than that of their contemporaries. Most Arts and Crafts pottery is thrown rather than molded, as mentioned above. Additionally, Rookwood not only explored a variety of styles, but often produced them concurrently. For example, during the decade the firm made Arts and Crafts–styled ware, they were also working in Iris glaze and Sea Green (Art Nouveau), Standard glaze (Victorian), and Vellum glaze (Impressionism). Any truly serious Arts and Crafts pottery, like Grueby or Newcomb College, was working strictly in that style. This disparity said more about Rookwood's marketing acumen than it did about its commitment to the period.

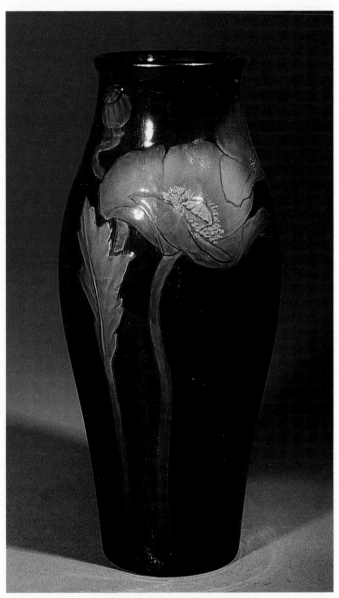

Maker: *Matthew A. Daly*
Date Made: *1900*
Dimension: *14" tall*
Value: *$25,000–35,000*

Art Nouveau-styled Rookwood at its best. The surface of the vase is also carved in relief, but the bright colors, black ground, and glossy finish are all in contrast to a more subdued Arts and Crafts sensibility.

Painted Matte

Painted matte is Rookwood's most successful matte-glazed line, though it is stylistically inconsistent with nearly every other American ceramic of the period. Also called the two-step process, artists painted decoration, almost always floral, in matte glazes on a contrasting (usually single-color) ground. Both the background and the decoration were actually painted in overglaze, rather than in slip relief beneath an overglaze, thus omitting the usual third glazing step and the attendant third firing.

This was a tricky technique to master because the rich matte glazes ran during firing, often blurring decoration well beyond what was originally intended. Some examples that were closer to

a kiln wall or in a kiln hot spot ran unevenly from side to side, resulting in a pot that was half perfect and half unrecognizable.

Nevertheless, at their best, painted matte pieces possess an inner luminosity and a softness of detail that is unmatched in American ceramics. You can compare Rookwood's work with that of the Valentien Pottery in San Diego and the Walrath Pottery in Rochester, New York, both of which worked at least occasionally in a similar style and technique. They were seldom as successful as Rookwood, at least in this regard.

The best Rookwood pieces have sharply contrasting colors between the decoration and the background. Usually, the best of these have more than a single color in the decoration. Oddly, the pieces are often better when depicting flowers with larger petals, such as poppies, because the nature of the decoration, which is at least slightly diffused in even the best of examples, often obliterates the fine detailing of more articulated blossoms, such as chrysanthemums.

Maker: *Olga G. Reed*
Date Made: *1906*
Dimension: *10" tall*
Value: *$8,000–10,000*

Another fine piece of painted matte. The floral design benefits from a nearly perfect firing.

Maker: *H. E. Wilcox*
Date Made: *1905*
Dimension: *8" tall*
Value: *$13,000–17,000*

An exceptional example of painted matte ware, luminous in color, decorated in polychrome on a burnt rose ground.

Maker: *Sara Sax*
Date Made: *1904*
Dimension: *4" tall*
Value: *$2,500–3,500*

Cabinet-sized painted matte, again showing a richness of color and simplicity of design that makes this line a collector favorite.

Perfectly fired pieces are really quite rare, and many of the best ones have been under ten inches tall. In truth, they are so lovely, and so very different from most other Arts and Crafts work, any serious collector would welcome a perfect example in just about any size. That this was a difficult decorative technique is illustrated by the limited number of artists who used it to any effect. Successful artists included Sara Sax, Olga G. Reed, Albert Valentien, and Kataro Shirayamadani.

As with nearly all Rookwood, even minor damage will reduce a piece's worth by about 50 percent. It is my contention that a great piece of Rookwood with a neat drill through the base should always be bought at no less than half of what it would bring otherwise. These pieces seem like bargains to me at that price, and this sort of damage has the least impact on the beauty and condition of a piece. Even though the market has proved me wrong on this point, I continue to hope that the smart money seeks these out.

Incised, Carved, and Modeled Mattes

Frankly, *incised, carved,* and *modeled* are probably the correct names for these lines only in the way they describe the decorative process. Since I'm an old pottery dog, I'm resistant to accepting new, or more recently discovered old, names of Rookwood lines. I'm assuming you'll forgive me as long as we both know what I'm talking about.

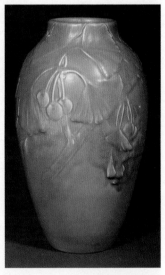

Maker: *Kataro Shirayamadani*
Date Made: *1905*
Dimension: *11" tall*
Value: *$8,000–12,000*

Ovoid vase with gingko leaves and berries and rich matte green as a finish. Fully carved vases by this master are extremely rare.

The bulk of Rookwood's Arts and Crafts ware is matte-glazed pieces with tooled and painted designs on contrasting grounds. Some artists, such as William Hentschel, usually incised designs into the clay body, allowing the background color to fill in the

Maker: *Charles Todd*
Date Made: *ca 1905*
Dimension: *12" tall*
Value: *$3,500–4,500*

A more typical, if unexceptional, carved matte vase. This piece benefits from the use of five rich, contrasting glazes and a heavy carving hand. While the form might be a bit tame, the rest of the pot more than compensates.

negative space. He chose other colors for his decorations, which were almost always flowers. It is important to be selective about the glazing of this ware, which at its best can incorporate some of the most complex and vibrant matte finishes used by this company. The incising and/or modeling are often muted so you should look for pieces with at least two or three contrasting but complementary colors. Most of these have dark backgrounds, but the best of them are often on medium tones such as caramel brown, ochre, or rose.

Other artists, like Charles Todd, were more inclined to lightly carve or incise the ceramic surface, creating subtle layers of decoration, both above and below the original body. Look for sharp detailing, an interplay of depth, and maximum coverage of decoration rather than designs restricted to a small portion of the pot. Also, single-color pieces, such as the ones often created by Albert Pons, can be very dull. The best often employ at least three or four contrasting glazes.

Condition is again a serious issue when buying either of the two lines described above. A single chip can easily reduce value by at least 50 percent.

Maker: *Charles Todd*
Date Made: *ca 1905*
Dimension: *13" tall*
Value: *$2,500–3,500*

This is a very typical incised matte. Note how the design is merely outlined rather than carved. And, though the glazes are really quite good, they do not offer a great deal of contrast. Finally, only about 30 percent of the surface is decorated.

Figurals

Finally, artists such as Anna Maria Valentien hand-sharpened their molded figural vases much in the style of Artus Van Briggle, who worked at Rookwood and left a year or two before the firm fully embraced this sort of ware. These pieces often lack the grace and freedom shown in Van Briggle's work in Colorado Springs, but there are examples that occasionally echo that master's success. Also, the glazing Rookwood used was often quite static, opting for mostly single matte glazes, usually lacking in depth. These are lovely pieces nonetheless and, if you choose to collect them, pay attention to the quality of the glazing; the molded blanks are consistently very good so they are much less an issue.

Maker: *Albert Valentien*
Date Made: *ca 1905*
Dimension: *6" tall*
Value: *$5,000–7,000*

Exceptional Rookwood figural of a dancing woman with a flowing skirt. Rich mustard matte finish.

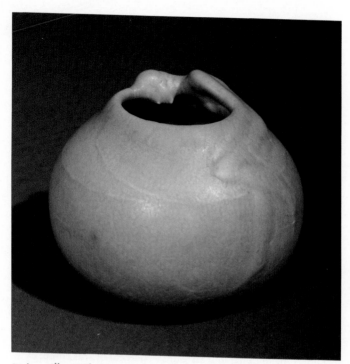

Maker: *Albert Valentien*
Date Made: *1901*
Dimension: *3" tall*
Value: *$1,500–2,500*

Another figural by Valentien, though this one is more subtle in design and glaze.

Because of the high-relief decoration that typifies this line, minor damage on ridges and peaks are not a big problem. Minor roughness and nicks on the best of these might reduce value by 10 to 20 percent, but such pieces are rare enough that they remain quite salable in spite of flaws.

Bottom of Rookwood vase with matte glazing and company logo.

Saturday Evening Girls/ Paul Revere Pottery

SATURDAY EVENING GIRLS/PAUL REVERE POTTERY IS ONE OF THE MORE EMOTIONALLY CHARGED AND PECULIAR POTTERIES OF THE ARTS AND CRAFTS PERIOD. Nearly their entire output consisted of utilitarian ware, focusing on plates, bowls, porridge sets, and mugs.

To further complicate matters, most of their ware was undecorated, coated only in their signature enamel, semigloss finishes. Added to the mix is the problem that, even though they remained in operation until the 1930s, nearly all of their best work was made prior to about 1915.

I don't mean to harshly discount 95 percent of this company's production: even their dullest pieces have a quality and charm found nowhere else in the American art pottery. Nevertheless, since this book is an exploration of the best decorative ceramics produced in this period, it serves us to look only at the small percentage of pieces that define the acme of their work.

I'll be more specific in a moment but, for now, you can immediately ignore pieces that are undecorated or those that have designs that cover only a small portion of the pot's surface. For example, some of their dinner and luncheon plates are covered primarily in single-enamel glazes. The decorated area might consist of a medallion in the plate's center, perhaps the size of a half-dollar coin, showing a stylized landscape or random water bird. For the advanced collector, this will hold your attention for about two minutes.

Further, after the company changed its name to the Paul Revere Pottery, nearly all pieces bearing this mark are simply not as good. I have seen a handful of pieces dated after 1920 that are worthy of any collection. Ultimately, we have to judge each piece on the beauty of its decoration and the overall workmanship. But there is no escaping the truth that their later work was almost always lacking in attractiveness and craft.

Date Made: *1925*
Dimension: *9" tall*
Value: *$7,000–8,000*

Paul Revere vase with iris in cuerda seca. *Decorated vase forms in both SEG and Paul Revere are rare. This one bears the characteristics of a later piece made by a looser hand that displays less stark coloration. Nevertheless, this example remains one of the best pieces from the Paul Revere period to come to market.*

Maker: *Fannie Levine*
Date Made: *1914*
Dimension: *11¼" diameter*
Value: *$35,000–45,000*

Large and early SEG centerpiece bowl decorated with geese in cuerda seca *in polychrome, on a yellow ground. While larger pieces of decorated SEG occasionally surface, they are seldom seen with such crisp, overall decoration.*

More important are larger pieces (vases, centerpiece bowls, large plates) or service pieces, such as covered casseroles. There are always exceptions, such as a porridge bowl with a fully decorated interior design. But, as with nearly all of our potteries, larger pieces with covering, bold decoration are best.

Decorative Styles

SEG/Paul Revere primarily employed three styles of decoration. *Cuerda seca,* or burnt rope technique, is one where designs are outlined in black, neatly separating the area of color within

Date Made: *1916*
Dimension: *6" tall*
Value: *$4,000–6,000*

Most SEG pieces are utilitarian in nature. This decorated wall pocket is unusual in form, and even more so as a result of the quality of decoration and its unique design. The crispness of execution is typical of the firm's earlier work.

Maker: *E. Brown*
Date Made: *ca 1925*
Dimension: *13" tall*
Value: *$18,000–22,000*

Paul Revere tall vase with butter-fat glazing, showing a stylized landscape. By the time this pot was made, the company's better days were long behind them. This piece shows that it is best to evaluate art by what you see rather than what you expect to be good.

Maker: *Fannie Goldstein*
Date Made: *1910*
Dimension: *5" diameter*
Value: *$8,000–10,000*

An even earlier work by SEG, this cereal bowl has the dry, hard enamel surface of their earliest pieces. The motto, typical of the Arts and Crafts period, increases interest and value.

the decoration. The enamel colors in the designs are slightly raised, giving the pieces subtle texture and strong definition. This ware is their most sought-after work and is usually found on earlier examples.

The second technique is an enamel painting much in the way of *cuerda seca,* but without the delineation of the design elements. Considering the limitations of glaze firing, when a little too much heat can cause the decoration to blur, such pieces seldom have the clarity of ware produced using the earlier, finer technique.

Finally, after about 1920, Paul Revere experimented with a rich, butterfat enamel that added great texture to the decorative surface. These are exceptions to the rule that were subject to the rudeness of the kiln. Well-fired examples of this butterfat glaze are extremely rare and account for nearly all of their best later work.

Maker: *Sarah Galner*
Date Made: *1913*
Dimension: *8" diameter*
Value: *$2,500–3,500*

This SEG closed bowl is well designed, though the iris blossoms and leaves are restricted to the upper rim. The best examples have decorations that cover nearly the entire surface of the vessel.

Decorative Elements

Not only are the designs chosen for a piece important, but how much of the surface those designs ultimately cover is also critical. For example, a well-decorated SEG piece will nearly always have a border motif of, say, a stylized landscape or a stylized water lily. These are fine as far as they go, but they are quite modest on a vessel where the entire exterior of a pot is covered in the round with a full landscape.

Much of SEG decorated ware was expertly produced so the question is seldom one of artistic quality. Whether the decoration consists of a gaggle of geese or a colony of rabbits, the larger the design elements, the better. It is for this reason that their taller and more fully decorated pieces have an unusual completeness to them.

The best motifs include landscapes, large flowers such as chrysanthemums, and vignettes with written mottoes such as "To the Steady Goes the Race."

Maker: *Sarah Galner*

Date Made: *1913*

Dimension: *8" tall*

Value: *$3,500–4,500*

One of the rarest pieces of SEG, this light sconce was made to fit over a standard candle or bulb holder. Note how the entire exposed surface is decorated. Further, the design is rendered in a tight cuerda seca of many colors, showing a full landscape. One of their rarest and best subjects.

Glazing

I am not sure what technical modifications the pottery experienced by about 1915, but their glazes changed at that time, and not for the better. Their earliest period, also known as their bowl shop period, employed eggshell-like enamel matte finishes that were hard and porous and extremely fine. Once you train your eyes, you can pick one of these pieces out from a breakfast table full of even slightly later work.

Date Made: *1926*
Dimension: *5" tall*
Value: *$1,500–2,000*

This piece of SEG is better than most of what is out there, but there are several things that make it less than exceptional. First, the size and form are fairly standard. The decoration is restricted to the top rim. Finally, the decoration is just surface painted and shows none of the delineation of their sharpest work.

Pieces from the mid-teens through about 1920 are also well glazed, but they lack the subtlety of the pottery's earliest work. This is yet another reason why the best pieces of SEG were nearly always made prior to about 1914.

Condition Issues

SEG/Paul Revere ware is relatively low fired, thin of body, and nearly always meant for table use. Consequently, damage is frequent even if limited to rim chips and short rim hairlines. One can only imagine the number of pieces that have shattered over the years, having been knocked from the table over breakfast.

Nevertheless, even minor flaws greatly reduce value on all but the best of pieces. That said, if you find one of their masterworks in just about any condition, you should consider it for your collection. They made precious few of these in the first place, and even fewer remain today.

One piece, a large bulbous vase, with *cuerda seca* chrysanthemums covering nearly the entire surface, was found a few decades back with a drill hole through its side. This pot, even with a surface drill, would still set a record deep into five figures were it to hit the market today.

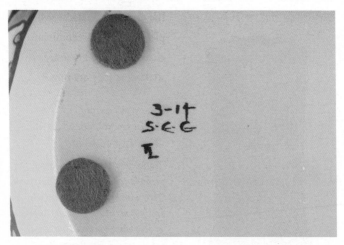

SEG mark, dated 1914.

Teco Pottery

TECO IS ONE OF THE ODDER ARTS AND CRAFTS COMPANIES. Nearly all of their pots were molded rather than hand thrown, with some of their most arresting forms appearing to be far more Art Nouveau than hardcore mission or Prairie School. Either because of or in spite of this, Teco has been a favorite of advanced collectors for decades. We'll examine different kinds of Teco ware, analyzing what separates the best from the rest.

Glazing is a very easy aspect of this company's work to evaluate. While they worked in a number of porous matte colors, including green, yellow, dark and light blue, maroon, cream, and slate gray, the best and most desirable is green. Unlike Grueby's matte greens, Teco's green varied little from piece to piece and was less organic in feel.

There are a number of Teco greens that were augmented with the addition of a charcoal black overglaze. These are nearly always better than the pieces without the overglaze. More often than not, the decorator used this secondary glaze to highlight the negative space of pieces with handles or embossed decoration, bringing out

the detail work. Rarer still are pieces that are predominantly charcoal black. These are as striking as they are rare.

Date Made: *ca 1905*
Dimension: *12" tall*
Value: *$3,500–4,500*

Notice how the charcoal-black secondary glazing on this floriform Teco vase brings out the details in the body of the pot. The addition of this black glaze almost always improves the visual appeal of these pieces.

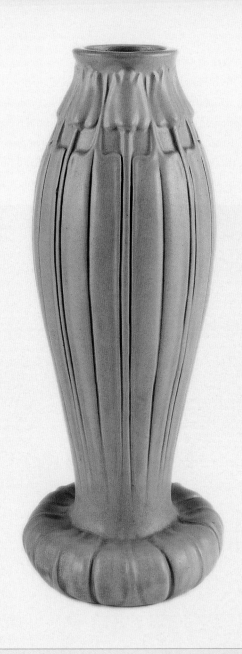

Date Made: *ca 1905*
Dimension: *14" tall*
Value: *$18,000–22,000*

*Fine Teco "tulip" vase with attenuated, embossed tulips
on an undulating blank. One of the company's more
unusual and seductive forms. These pieces are quite rare.*

Nouveau Forms

Some of Teco's best and most expensive work are pieces with curving, whiplash handles and/or embossed floral designs. With the exception of several small and dull pieces, you'll recognize one of these if you're fortunate enough to get a shot at one. Though molded, there must have been a fair amount of hand finishing because these would not have survived removal from a slip mold.

Date Made: *ca 1905*
Dimension: *10" tall*
Value: *$20,000–30,000*

Another exceptional piece of Teco pottery, with both embossed floral design and applied handles, under a green and charcoal matte finish.

Date Made: *ca 1905*
Dimension: *15" tall*
Value: *$70,000–80,000*

A masterpiece by any standard, this simple vase form is embellished with a series of whiplash handles encircling the bottom of the pot.

Perhaps it is for this reason, along with their fragility, that so few survive today.

In truth, advanced collectors are happy to have these in nearly any condition. There are only a handful of such forms and seldom are they found without at least minor damage. Also, because of their beauty and scarcity, one shouldn't be too picky about the quality of matte green, with or without charcoaling, that covers them.

Date Made: *ca 1905*
Dimension: *7" tall*
Value: *$1,500–2,500*

A typical Arts and Crafts example, with buttressed handles over a double gourd form. This piece came in several sizes, the largest measuring nearly fourteen inches tall.

Arts and Crafts Forms

Major pieces of Arts and Crafts Teco are far more common than whiplash Art Nouveau examples, though they represent less than 1 percent of the company's production. Bear in mind that Teco developed and produced thousands of molded forms and, generally speaking, these pieces are considered neither rare nor exceptional.

However, larger pieces, those over twelve inches in height, are scarce. The addition of chunky handles and/or deeply embossed rectilinear designs are the elements that contribute to a museum-quality piece. Because these are less prone to serious damage than Teco's organic work, and since they're somewhat easier to locate, the quality of glazing is slightly more a factor.

Date Made: *ca 1905*
Dimension: *6" tall*
Value: *$2,500–3,500*

Notice the Prairie School influences apparent in this piece. It has angular buttresses and a more horizontal flow. Bowls are typically not sought by advanced collectors, but this one is an exception to the rule.

Date Made: *ca 1905*
Dimension: *15" tall*
Value: *$13,000–17,000*

This massive, "architectonic" vase is yet another Teco masterpiece. The charcoaling in the lowlights of the handles reinforces the vertical lines of the pot.

Date Made: *ca 1905*
Dimension: *5" tall*
Value: *$750–1,250*

An example of the firm's yellow matte finish.

Date Made: *ca 1905*
Dimension: *9" tall*
Value: *$2,500–3,500*

A blue matte vase on one of Teco's weirder forms.

Date Made: *ca 1905*
Dimension: *13" tall*
Value: *$1,800–2,200*

While some of Teco's non-green pots are worthy of consideration, the white matte finish is probably their least desirable glaze.

Date Made: *ca 1905*
Dimension: *7" tall*
Value: *$1,800–2,200*

Teco's matte brown finish is second in popularity only to their trademark green.

Minor damage on a major Art Nouveau piece reduces value by about 10 percent. A few chips to the edges of a handle or buttress on an Arts and Crafts piece might reduce value by about 25 percent. Teco is nearly always marked at least once with their trademark die-stamped cipher.

One more note concerns the color of the glazing: while collectors pay premium prices for matte green pots, you should not avoid major pieces in one of their other finishes. In fact, you could buy a masterpiece, rarer in a color other than green, for perhaps two-thirds of what you would pay otherwise.

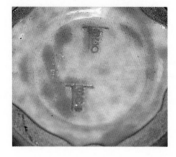

The firm's die-stamped mark.

Tiffany Pottery

LOUIS COMFORT TIFFANY'S POTTERY IS ONE OF THE
STRANGER ARTS AND CRAFTS OFFERINGS. Tiffany was a
design genius by any standard, famous for his lighting, decorative glass, enamels, and metalwork. That pottery was something
of an afterthought for him is apparent in the unevenness of his

Date Made: *ca 1910*
Dimension: *7" tall*
Value: *$1,800–2,200*

*Lamp base form with a metallic brown flambé. One of the reasons Tiffany
introduced a ceramic line was to provide lamp bases for his leaded glass
shades. They are usually of good to very good quality but are seldom among
the firm's best pieces of art pottery.*

Date Made: *ca 1910*
Dimension: *8" tall*
Value: *$25,000–35,000*

Tiffany footed compote with embossed reeds and frogs under a green glossy finish. Arguably Tiffany's best piece of art pottery, this example is well designed and covered with one of the firm's best glazes.

work. Much of his art pottery was intended to serve as lamp bases for some of his leaded shades. There are also a number of his freestanding hollowware vessels on the market today. We'll examine both types of his pottery here.

Lamp Bases

Tiffany's lamp bases were often molded, but I've seen a number of thrown examples. Either way, they are often large and cumbersome, appearing incomplete without the fittings and shades that were originally intended. The glazing on these bases is usually more extravagant than on his other vases, often with flowing matte crystalline finishes of blue or green and flowing flambés in brown. Look for bigger pieces with handles, bearing one of Tiffany's more exciting glazes.

Date Made: *ca 1910*
Dimension: *6" tall*
Value: *$4,000–6,000*

Perhaps half of the Tiffany pottery that exists today is found in a bisque-fired white clay exterior with a glossy green interior. While the quality of these pieces is uniformly very good, they seldom rank among Tiffany's most important pieces. This reticulated example with embossed apple blossoms is fine as far as it goes. However, unless you're building a comprehensive collection of the firm's work, it would be better to wait for one covered with their trademark glazing.

Pottery

Tiffany Pottery is far more successful in vase form, though there are a disproportionate number of dull examples. The main reason is that at least half of them were never coated with an outer glaze, leaving them a chalky white bisque on the exterior, with an apple green high gloss on the interior (perhaps to discourage sweating if used for flowers). Few of Tiffany's designs were strong enough to carry the pieces without one of his small selection of overglazes.

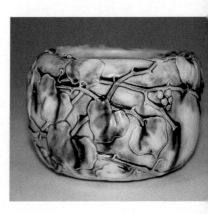

Date Made: *ca 1910*
Dimension: *7" tall*
Value: *$7,000–8,000*

A very good piece, with embossed fruit and leaves under a green-and-"shellac"-yellow finish.

The best of the pots have embossed floral and/or leaf designs in high relief, covered with one of several of his trademark finishes. There are a few forms with embossed lizards or frogs, but the majority are strictly vegetal. They tend to be small, with 90 percent of his non-lamp-base vases measuring less than eleven inches in height. The best of these are reticulated through the pot's body, covered from top to bottom with embossed work, ending unevenly at the top rim, shaped by the irregularity of the blossoms.

Date Made: *ca 1910*
Dimension: *7" tall*
Value: *$2,500–3,500*

A curious piece of Tiffany pottery with an excellent blue-and-green flambé over an unusual rectangular blank.

Date Made: *ca 1910*
Dimension: *7" tall*
Value: *$3,500–4,500*

Displaying a particularly good glaze on an above-average blank, this stick vase is decorated with embossed tulips under a dynamic flambé.

The most common glazes are a gloss to semigloss green, usually with patches of cream, or shellac yellow–brown with a similar mottling to white. While these are not the most interesting glazes used by America's Arts and Crafts potters, they are somehow satisfying in Tiffany's work.

Because Tiffany's shape selection was somewhat limited, and because the better pots are almost always molded, minor damage will reduce value greatly on all but the best of pieces. Pots are nearly always marked, usually with the LCT cipher incised into the bottom center. Occasionally, other scratched-in designations, such as *favrille pottery,* will accompany the company's cipher.

It is worth pointing out that, because the mark is so easy to copy, there are a great number of Tiffany fakes circulating through the market. Less available, though still worthy of concern, are a number of genuine Tiffany bisque vases with glazes or finishes added after factory. I have seen between five and ten such pieces that were simply spray-painted gold.

An authentic LCT cipher incised into the bottom of a bisque-fired pot.

Date Made: *ca 1910*
Dimensions: *8″ tall*
Value: *$8,000–12,000*

A fine organic vase with embossed wisteria pods with an unusual rich green semigloss finish. This is a fine piece of Tiffany pottery.

Van Briggle Pottery

THE POTTERY MADE BY ARTUS AND ANNA VAN BRIGGLE IN COLORADO SPRINGS HAS BEEN A FAVORITE OF AMERICAN COLLECTORS FOR DECADES. This work is at once romantic, sensual, and blessed with sufficient production to allow for a broad collecting base.

The pottery went through many changes and is the only period company to remain in operation through today. It might seem that, with over a century of ceramic production, it would be difficult to sift through it to distinguish the best. This is far from the case, however, as each subsequent period of production was somewhat weaker than the previous.

Following are the different eras of the Van Briggle Pottery.

1901–1904: the first and most important time of production at the Van Briggle Pottery. Artus, who was in Colorado Springs because he was suffering from tuberculosis, died in 1904. Most of the best pottery was made while he was still alive.

1905–1907: the period just after Artus's death when Anna was in full control of the pottery, keeping it alive

Date Made: *1902*
Dimension: *12" tall*
Value: *$13,000–17,000*

A large, bulbous vase from the firm's earliest period. At its best, Van Briggle's work is matte painted in more than one color. Because matte glazes tended to run in the kiln, the best examples show enough "feathering" without loss of detail to the embossed designs.

Date Made: *ca 1906*
Dimension: *13" tall*
Value: *$13,000–17,000*

*A most beautiful example of Van Briggle's early work.
While this is a molded pot, there is considerable sharpening
to the molded design. In addition, the glazing has a nacreous
luster that works well with the conventionalized design.*

Date Made: *1907*
Dimension: *15" tall*
Value: *$9,000–11,000*

From the period just after Van Briggle's death, this vase shows the firm's new direction under Anna Van Briggle's management. This tall vase relies less on secondary glazing. It instead relies on the dark clay color to become part of the design. The detailing of the molded decoration during this period usually results in sharper edges around the flowers or, in this case, peacock feathers.

in his name. Pieces from this time were consistently good to very good. Relatively few masterpieces were produced during these years, however.

1908–1912: the last era of consistently fine work at the pottery. While occasional masterworks were made during this time, most pieces suffered from watered-down designs, lighter molds, and inconsistent glazing.

1913–1915: the brief period when businessmen, taking over after Anna's departure, produced a respectable ware with occasional flashes of inspiration. Mostly, pieces pale in comparison with the pottery's earliest production.

Date Made: *1910*
Dimension: *15" tall*
Value: *$5,500–6,500*

This pot was made just prior to Anna Van Briggle's sale of the company to outside businessmen. While still an imposing example, note both the relative weakness of the design and the thinness of the glazing. This is about as good a 1910 piece as one could expect, but it is not on par with their earlier work.

Date Made: *1914*
Dimension: *7" tall*
Value: *$1,800–2,200*

While not clearly dated, this piece is probably from 1914. This is one of the few pieces made after Anna's departure that bears some trace of the pottery's earlier glory.

Date Made: *ca 1925*
Dimension: *16" tall*
Value: *$1,800–2,200*

Dating from about 1925, this is better than most other American art pottery made at this time, but it is a far cry from their earlier efforts. The design is weak and the glaze typical. The piece is more a comment on how far their work had fallen.

1916–1925: a time of consistently good production pottery, but, even at their best, these pieces seemed more like tourist ware aimed at keeping the kilns firing than in defining a superior ceramic.

1926–1932: Van Briggle's last period of production bearing any resemblance to the early golden years.

Date Made: *pre-1932*
Dimension: *15" tall*
Value: *$1,000–2,000*

Made just prior to 1932, this is a great example of Depression-era art pottery. It is a reprise of an early and great form. But, once again, the pot suffers from a weak mold and predictable glazing.

Glazes

One could fuel an ongoing argument over whether Van Briggle's glazes or their Art Nouveau/Arts and Crafts-inspired forms were more important. Clearly, their best work possesses a combination of the two. Van Briggle championed the use of rich vegetal mattes that were a vital part of the Arts and Crafts aesthetic.

It should come as no surprise that the most common color employed at Van Briggle during the early years was green. From about 1901 until about 1912, they developed perhaps a dozen different matte greens, and these were used alone or in tandem with other hues.

Date Made: *1904*
Dimension: *9" tall*
Value: *$4,000–5,000*

Another beautifully glazed early piece of Van Briggle in matte brown tones.

Date Made: *1903*
Dimension: *11" tall*
Value: *$4,500–5,500*

A fine early vase decorated with two different matte green finishes. Note the sharpness of the mold even when glazed with a thick, flowing finish. Also, the earlier glazes were much more complex, showing much activity in the kiln.

Date Made: *1905*
Dimension: *8" tall*
Value: *$1,800–2,200*

Though slightly later, this pot shows crisp modeling of the mold and excellent glazing.

Other early colors worthy of consideration are a rich ochre and deep black; dark blues and purples; and the early version of their mulberry, or burgundy, finish. Most pieces were glazed in a single color. Pots with second or third glazes adorning embossed floral designs and leaves are usually better. Such multiglazed pieces, however, often show the same problems other companies experienced in painting with matte finishes: the finishes often ran in the firing, resulting in blurry flowers and mushy definition.

Date Made: *1903*
Dimension: *9" tall*
Value: *$2,500–3,500*

While some overfired pieces can be attractive, it is always better if the matte glazing stays somewhere in the vicinity of the decoration. This example shows more color run than is commonly acceptable by advanced collectors.

What was even more important than the color of a pot was how well the piece was treated by the kiln. Unlike many of the other Arts and Crafts companies, such as Grueby, whose matte glazes were hard and even, Van Briggle "pulled" or "feathered" glazes, gathering the surface so that the glazing was denser in some areas and thin (to the point of exposing clay or becoming lighter due to the clay's influence) in others. These varied effects, while not unique to Van Briggle pottery, were seldom achieved with such success elsewhere.

Date Made: *1905*
Dimension: *7" tall*
Value: *$1,300–1,700*

Another overfired piece of early Van Briggle, the defect is somewhat concealed by the use of a single color. Nevertheless, the glazing has the effect of minimizing the embossed decoration.

Decoration

Van Briggle pottery was almost entirely molded ware, so there is fair repetition of form. It is worth mentioning that the pottery fired hard and pieces are usually found with little to no post-manufacturing damage. As a result, we have been blessed with a fair sampling of what the company produced in these early years.

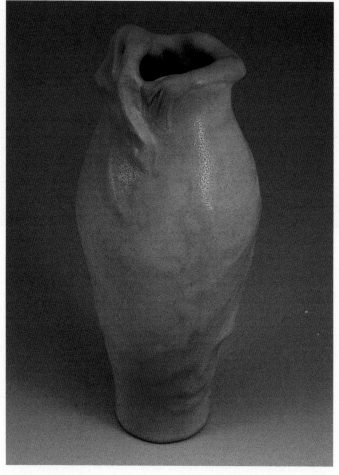

Date Made: *1902*
Dimension: *10" tall*
Value: *$22,000–28,000*

A Van Briggle classic, this early Lorelai *vase is the firm's signature piece, showing a diaphanously clad woman in repose. Note the use of more than one glaze, which is very rare on the early versions of this form.*

Date Made: *1902*
Dimension: *13" tall*
Value: *$22,000–28,000*

One of the firm's rarest early figural vases. The Lady of the Lily motif was continued through later years, but those examples have only served to give the concept a bad name. The thin microcrystalline glazing allows for sharp detailing.

Both Artus and Anna Van Briggle were sculptors at heart, and they adorned a majority of their early work with rich organic designs. These motifs were a combination of Art Nouveau flourishes and stylized Arts and Crafts ideas. I have seen a few early examples that, though molded, were left unglazed. It was clear that a certain amount of "sharpening" of the mold was done with hand tools to strengthen details that would often blur in the mold, especially with repeated use. Molds did not last forever and, eventually, embossed designs lost their crispness.

The designs are usually floral, animal, or human in nature. The best embrace the entirety of the piece. Geometric designs seldom have the same grace. The Van Briggles made a series of pots with human forms, and the most important of these are their signature pieces, the *Despondency* and the *Lorelai*. The former is a tall, masculine pot with a man's figure draped around the top, his legs dangling into the body of the vase. The latter shows a diaphanously clad woman who literally envelops most of the pot's surface. These should be considered trademark examples, especially if dated prior to Artus's death.

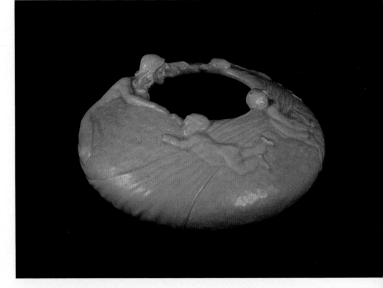

Date Made: *1902*
Dimension: *9″ diameter*
Value: *$30,000–40,000*

The only example known of this early figural showing a woman and several cherubs amid a swirling ground in rich, feathered matte green.

Date Made: *1902*
Dimension: *8" tall*
Value: *$18,000–22,000*

Another important and early Van Briggle figural Dos Cabezos, rendered with strong Art Nouveau lines under a rich and flowing matte blue glaze.

Other figural pieces include *Climbing for Honey,* a vase with two bears scaling the sides of a tall pot, and the *Lily of the Valley,* with a naked woman adjacent to a large, open blossom. While exceptional pieces in their own right, neither is as emotionally charged as the *Despondency* or the *Lorelai.* The Van Briggles knew that Artus's days were numbered, and these two pieces are a testament of their doomed love.

Larger early florals are also extremely rare. The average Van Briggle vase is about seven to eight inches in height, and exceptional ones easily measure over a foot tall. I have seen taller ones still, with some approaching twenty inches. But these tend to be somewhat later and seldom possess the visual intensity of their earliest work.

As mentioned earlier, Van Briggle ware has a hard, dense body and is pleasantly resistant to damage. Because of this, and since molded forms were repeated, damage greatly reduces value.

The bottom of an early Van Briggle vase. This is typical of the undersides of pieces made prior to Artus's death in 1904.

The bottom of an early pot made in 1906 after Artus's death.

Walley Pottery

WALLEY POTTERY, WHICH WAS LOCATED IN STERLING JUNCTION, MASSACHUSETTS, is about as Arts and Crafts a producer as you'll find, even if much of William Walley's work is unexciting. Walley said that there was more quality in a "brick hand formed and fired by a single artist than in the best piece of molded ware ever made." As you might expect with such a proclamation, Walley ware is hand thrown in the worst of cases.

Once again, since we're using the standard set by Grueby, evaluating Walley pieces must come down to assessing form and glazing. Size is also a factor, but most of Walley's pieces were smallish, with anything over ten inches tall being considered large. The last consideration is the overall quality of the piece. Since each of Walley's pots was truly a unique piece of art he, like his spiritual compatriot George Ohr, had good days and bad days.

Date Made: *ca 1910*
Dimension: *5" tall*
Value: *$1,800–2,200*

Unusual two-color Walley vase with rich blue matte leaves on a fine green matte ground.

Date Made: *ca 1910*
Dimension: *15" tall*
Value: *$6,000–8,000*

Tall and exceptional Walley vase from the G. Koster Collection. This example is unusual in size, glazing, and modeling. The long handles serve as buttresses, and they are defined both by the modeling and the secondary glazing. Few pieces of Walley possess this much visual and structural strength.

Forms

Most Walley pieces are simply thrown, bulbous pots of red clay. The majority of these do not have tooled and applied, or modeled, decoration. The best shapes are of baluster form with closed rims and tapering bottoms. As stated earlier, these pieces tend to be small in size, the average less than eight inches in height.

Date Made: *ca 1910*
Dimension: *5" x 7"*
Value: *$1,100–1,500*

This squat, bulbous vase is very typical of most of Walley's pottery. It is a fine pot, as far as it goes, but it lacks the modeled decoration and rich glazing that represent the best of his work.

Date Made: *ca 1910*
Dimension: *7" tall*
Value: *$1,300–1,700*

This is a better-than-average example of this artist's work. Not only is the body of the pot decorated with modeled leaves, but there are heavily worked, applied handles. The green matte is typical of his better glazes.

Decoration

Decorated Walley pieces are fairly rare. The best of them show modeled designs of leaves enveloping the surfaces of pots. While the leaf decoration is strongly reminiscent of Grueby's work, Walley usually "beaded" the edges of their designs so that they were rounded and smooth instead of sharp, like Grueby's. Perhaps only one in eight Walley pots has tooled and applied decoration.

That said, the same criteria apply when evaluating the success of a decorated Walley pot. Usually, the more of the surface that is covered, the better. Further, the integration of decoration and form is important here. My own preference is for rounder pieces with leaves wrapping about the bulbous body, ending unevenly near the rim.

Date Made: *ca 1910*

A close-up of another vase with applied leaves, showing the rounder "beading" that often defined the edges of Walley's applied decoration.

Glazing

Walley had a limited range of glazes, and, like most of the Arts and Crafts potters, he tended towards green. Further, he usually employed a single overall color, with occasional beading around leaf edges in a reddish brown. Rarely, there are examples with the leaves in a color other than the one he used on the background. One such example shows blue leaves on a light green ground.

More importantly, Walley seemed, almost at random, to use gloss finishes in place of matte. My own preference, which is usually the case in matters of Arts and Crafts, is strictly for matte glazing. Successful finishes are usually in shades of green (the darker the better), though Walley also mixed a rich matte blue or brown.

Date Made: *ca 1910*
Dimension: *7" tall*
Value: *$1,000–1,400*

A most unusual flowing semigloss finish with a feathered matte green flambé.

Because Walley's work is one of a kind and since his better-decorated ware is scarce, minor damage does not severely reduce value. One should expect roughness on the edges of leaves as the low-fire biscuit was quick to chip around the edges.

The best piece of Walley is about eight inches tall, of bulbous form, with carved and applied leaves under a rich, dark, matte finish.

Date Made: *ca 1910*
Dimension: *6" tall*
Value: *$1,800–2,200*

Another fine example with tooled leaves and a semigloss finish.

Arts and Crafts Furniture

THERE ARE ONLY A FEW PEOPLE I CAN THINK OF WHO HAVE ACTUALLY AMASSED AN ENCYCLOPEDIC COLLECTION OF MISSION OAK FURNITURE. The rest of us are still furnishing our homes. For all of us, there was a starting point — that first rocker or armchair — that changed our lives forever. Since then, we have bought, sold, and traded to achieve the collection we will never be completely satisfied with. Unlike metalwork or ceramics, we can only collect a certain number of furniture pieces without our homes looking like warehouses.

As mentioned in the introduction to this book, the Arts and Crafts Movement in America 1876–1916, the seminal exhibition organized by the Princeton University Art Museum and the Art Institute of Chicago, was the starting point for the Arts and Crafts revival. Prior to this major 1972 exhibition, there were only a small number of people who recognized the importance of this period. This exhibit, which also traveled to the Renwick Gallery, in Washington, D.C., proved to the museum world the importance of this little-known period in the history of decorative arts.

There are many books that explain the historic importance of the Arts and Crafts period and how it began in England and spread to this country through social reform. But what attracted the collector in the 1960s and early '70s to this seemingly simple furniture? I believe it was some of the same reasons that the period began in the first place: the need to simplify our interiors and to surround ourselves with beautifully designed, well-proportioned, and expertly executed objects that feature the honest use of materials. Wood should look like wood and metal like metal.

The catalog The Arts and Crafts Movement in America 1876–1916, *published by Princeton University in 1972, accompanied the seminal exhibit of the same name at the Art Museum, Princeton University.*

During the early years of collecting, very few people held information on the material that would be collected over the next several decades. Slowly, however, period catalogs began to surface. I was very excited the day I received my photocopy of two Tobey Furniture catalogs, two *Chips from the Craftsman Workshops* catalogs, and the *Things Wrought from the Craftsman Workshops* catalog. (All of these catalogs have since been republished.) These catalogs and other sources helped collectors identify pieces they were searching for. Still, little was known about the volume of material or the scarcity of individual forms.

During these early years of collecting, prices varied widely across the country. They were highest in larger metropolitan areas due to a few pioneering dealers who saw and appreciated the potential of Arts and Crafts furniture. Discovering a rare piece of Gustav Stickley furniture at some remote flea market in upstate New York or even at the 26th Street Flea Market in New York City was not unheard of and for a while was even expected. Today, there is still that possibility, but instead of ten people looking, now there are hundreds. I remember shopping Brimfield and other outdoor markets and filling my van with some pretty good pieces and occasionally scoring some great pieces without spending much money. Supply and demand have a significant effect on today's prices.

I am often asked how I know what to look for. I also hear

questions such as, "What makes this rocker worth $300 and this one worth $3,000?" There are many variables to consider when evaluating a piece of Arts and Crafts furniture. Designer or manufacturer, form or function, when during the period it was produced, quality of materials used, and the condition of the piece are the main considerations. The more you study a piece, the more you will see and understand. Reading and comprehending the research that has been done is very important, but experiencing examples in person is essential.

Identifying the Maker

Identifying the designer or manufacturer is the starting point. Today, many catalog reprints with period photos or line drawings that include dimensions are available to help identify makers. These illustrations should be memorized, not necessarily the catalog numbers, but the forms. Refer to these catalogs frequently. Refer also to museum and gallery exhibition catalogs, general histories of the period, and histories of individual companies and craftsman.

Building a personal reference library is very important. I often buy two copies of research material, one as a working copy and

the second as a replacement for when the first one wears out. This research material will prove priceless in helping you learn to recognize forms.

Gustav Stickley's Craftsman Furnishings for the Home, *published October 1912.*

Stickley Brothers, Grand Rapids, Michigan. Paper label used early in their production, exact date unknown.

Many companies produced very similar forms. It is important to know who did what. Unlike pottery and metalwork, the marks used on furniture were primarily decals and paper labels that were vulnerable to all types of things. The use of branded marks made it easier for us.

Beware: the use of fraudulent marks is on the rise. Detecting a fake mark can be difficult. I have seen expertly applied new decals, and I have seen Xeroxed marks on off-colored paper glued to a surface and then shellacked over. The latter are pretty easy to detect. When you examine a piece of furniture, study the mark; look at the wood and finish around it. Studying original marks will help you develop an eye for spotting fakes.

Construction Methods

This was the beginning of the twentieth century and mass production and continuity were crucial to success. Knowing the difference between a through tenon, flush tenon, and keyed tenon, as well as the function of a spline is fundamental to the identification process. Manufacturers tended to adopt construction methods unique to their operation. Understanding these different construction techniques, as well as when and why they were used, will help.

The better companies used true construction without fake joinery embellishing the piece inappropriately. As a general rule, the period was about the honest use of materials, so when we find a piece of furniture with a tenon that is being held with a couple of small nails, our suspicion should be aroused.

There are some pretty good knockoffs. The hardware could be purchased from many of the better companies, and companies' plans were published. There were spinoff companies that took designs with them, companies that just outright copied, and talented technical school students ambitious enough to produce pieces like Stickley sideboards and Morris chairs well enough to fool most collectors.

Form and Function

The issue of form and design is subjective. Obviously different forms appeal to some people and not to others. I have watched many of my customers' personal tastes develop and understanding of the period grow with time and involvement. I believe that the most successful way to develop an eye for form is to look at as many pieces as possible. Visit public collections. There are many museums that have built collections and it is the responsibility of the museum curators to display what is either historically important or aesthetically superior in design.

Another way of learning is to attend auctions that specialize in the period. It is possible to view many examples in a very short period of time, allowing you the opportunity to touch and turn things over, thoroughly inspecting every piece. Pay attention to what things sell for. There is a reason that a Gustav Stickley eight-leg sideboard will consistently sell for three times what a Stickley Brothers sideboard does. I'm not saying that the Stickley Brothers sideboard is bad, just that the Gustav sideboard is better.

Doweled through tenon on a Gustav Stickley trumpet stretcher, used until 1904.

Keyed tenons found on an early Gustav Stickley bungalow table, ca 1903.

Flush tenon on a Gustav Stickley table, ca 1903.

Spline used on the top of a Stickley Brothers table.

GUSTAV STICKLEY MORRIS CHAIR

Maker: *United Crafts*

Date Made: *1902–1903*

Dimensions: *40" x 31¼" x 36"*

Value: *$10,000–$25,000*

Early Gustav Stickley Morris Chair, model number 2342.

When Produced

At what time furniture was produced is not a foremost concern if you're decorating or furnishing a home, but it is a major factor if you're building a collection. The furniture produced during the early years can be described as gutsy. This was a time of experimentation. Both exceptional and not-so-good examples were produced. As the period evolved so did the objects. Designs matured and changed, were added and dropped, some for the better and some for the worse.

Construction methods were revised to accommodate an increasing market and rising production costs. Towards the end of the period, many designs became watered down or the aesthetics completely changed, becoming more sensitive to the Art Deco or Colonial Revival periods that would eventually overtake Arts and Crafts.

Knowing what maker did what first is very important. This is critical because of the amount of copying done. For example, Gustav Stickley's flat-arm model number 2342 Morris chair, which was introduced early in 1902, was copied by many different companies. JM Young, L. and L. G. Stickley, and Lifetime Furniture Company produced very similar forms. Production furniture, being conducive to catalog sales and mass marketing, made it easy for companies to track each other's furniture lines.

Knowing who came first is also important when calculating the historic or monetary value of a piece. Become acquainted with the different variations of form made by the same company, and which variations were produced first. For instance, Gustav Stickley's flat-arm model number 2342 Morris chair was changed a couple of years after initially being offered. The catalog number was changed to 332, and this piece became nearly three inches longer from front to back. Subtle changes like this affect proportion and scale. These slight changes can mean the difference in value of thousands of dollars to collectors.

Materials

No matter what wood is used, the quality of the wood and other materials used will affect value. Pay attention to details since quality of materials can vary significantly. The primary and most desirable wood is quartersawn American white oak, exhibiting tight growth rings and well-defined rays. Wood is an organic material and there are no two boards alike. Quartersawn lumber displays the wood's ring structure on its wide surface, as well as figure and grain patterns to their best advantage. Cutting the log in this manner yields less wood, but the wood is of a higher quality, denser, and much more beautiful.

Early in the period and for a short time, chestnut, which has a very wide-open grain and is much less dense than oak, was used. That use of this wood was discontinued may have been connected to the blight that destroyed nearly all the chestnut in this country early in the century. Many companies offered mahogany and maple as well, although these woods were not as popular then nor are

Diagram of the way a log was milled to produce ray flake in a piece of oak.

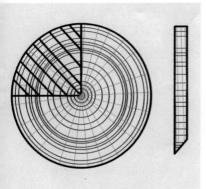

The distinct graining of quarter-sawn American white oak.

The distinct graining of American chestnut.

they now. These woods add a formality to furniture that works better with forms that haven't accentuated the construction, including inlay furniture that the Stickley Brothers Company produced and the production furniture that Harvey Ellis designed for Gustav Stickley. I have never seen a manufactured piece of cherry mission furniture.

Condition

Condition is the last variable. Ideally, look for original-condition, untouched pieces. Building a collection that can be described this way, however, is very difficult.

To understand condition, it is necessary to understand construction, finishes, and wood. All three work together and directly affect each other. As the quality of construction, finishes, and wood increase, the benefits of restoration likewise increase. Resurrecting a table from a damp basement becomes a viable option if the table is worth enough.

Determining if a piece has been altered is also increasingly more important. Become familiar with what new wood looks like and how to recognize wood filler. Dark waxes, stains, and other methods of disguise can be very difficult to detect.

Examine the bottoms of legs. When produced, most legs were given a slight bevel to eliminate the possibility of a leg chipping when being dragged across the floor. Subsequently, many objects were relegated to the basement or the garage. The damp floors caused wood to rot and become soft. The bottoms of legs is the primary place that a piece may be altered or repaired. End grain that is a hundred years old is porous, and many times a metal glide has been put in the bottom of the leg. Look for evidence of this. A freshly cut leg even twenty or more years old will display a tighter end grain with fresher color. This is an area where wood filler might be used as well. Look for discoloration and the lack of grain or subtle changes in the grain. Wood replacement is acceptable if you know the work was done and the furniture is priced accordingly.

Dutchman repair is another method. This is a spliced-in patch of wood to repair a screw hole or large chip. This is an acceptable method of repair, but ideally you should be informed when and why it was used.

Finishes are also an important aspect of evaluating condition. Original surfaces are becoming more and more significant as collections begin to mature. The term *original finish* enhances the value of a piece, whether at an auction or in a private sale.

GUSTAV STICKLEY MAGAZINE STAND
Maker: *United Crafts*
Date Made: *1902–1903*
Dimensions: *35" x 15" x 14"*
Value: *$8,000–12,000*

Magazine stand with original finish.

Recognizing a refinish takes time, and again, the more pieces you study, the more understanding of finishes you will have. Inspecting for finish restoration or refinishing is a tactile task involving sight, smell, and touch. Look for cross-grain sanding, minute drips, and runs of new finishes, lack of wear on expected areas, or an abnormal sheen. Smell the surface. New finishes emit odors while curing. Waxes are easily detectable by feeling the surface. Original surfaces shrink and move with age. The grain opens and the finish follows this. Studying pieces that you know for certain have an original finish will help you recognize pieces that have been refinished.

The terminology of describing a finish may be the most mystifying aspect of evaluation. Terms such as enhanced *original finish, original finish with color added,* and *overcoated original finish* can all be confusing. You'll learn to decipher this terminology with time and exposure. I have heard claims that a piece had an overcoat removed, leaving its original finish. Once something other than a pure wax product has been put on an original finish, it's overcoated. I have never seen an overcoat removed that has left an original finish entirely intact.

It is critical to preserve pieces that have original leather. These are becoming increasingly rarer. The conservation of leather is possible and you should seek out the advice of a professional restorer. If you come across a piece with good original leather, consider paying more than you normally would. There is nothing better than the mellow color of old leather to enhance your collection.

MORRIS CHAIR
Maker: *JM Young*
Date Made: *1905*
Dimensions: *42" x 31½" x 36"*
Value: *$4,000—6,000*

Morris Chair with original leather.

Craftsman Workshops

Gustav Stickley is considered by nearly every authority on the American Arts and Crafts movement to be a leader and spokesperson for the period. His *Craftsman* magazine was influential

Red decal used by Gustav Stickley, Craftsman Workshops, 1905–1912.

in spreading Arts and Crafts philosophies and introducing its readership to many of the ideals of this period. Articles were published on virtually every social aspect of interest at the onset of the twentieth century. For the first sixteen years of this new century, Gustav Stickley changed the furniture industry and the way we view our furniture and surroundings today.

Gustav's furniture is some of the most highly prized and sought after by collectors today. In 1981, David Cathers, the leading authority on Gustav Stickley, published *Furniture of the American Arts and Crafts Movement: Stickley and Roycroft Mission Oak*. In this book, Cathers categorized Gustav's different periods: 1898–1900 as his "experimental" period; 1900–1904 as his "first mission" period; 1904–1910 as his "mature production" period; and finally 1910-1916 as his "final mission" period. This has become an important guide for collectors.

The "experimental" and "first mission" periods are the most important and my

The Craftsman *published monthly by the Craftsman Publishing Company in New York City. Gustav Stickley was the editor.*

Branded mark used by Gustav Stickley, Craftsman Workshops, 1915.

personal favorites. During these six years, Gustav Stickley was developing a style he hoped would make life a more sensual experience. Many of his early pieces can be found with hand-cut dovetails and other benchmarks that lead one to believe that each piece was made by an individual and not on a production line. Gustav had original ideas, and although he was more of a businessman than a designer, he knew what he wanted and had a plan to achieve it.

There were many furniture manufacturers, motivated primarily by what people wanted and what they could sell, that produced very nice pieces. Gustav produced what he loved and what he wanted people to respond to. He did not come to this position overnight, and the history of his beginnings can be read in numerous books that have been published in the last thirty years. Gustav Stickley's business savvy and perseverance carried him to the top within a few years.

TEA TABLE
Maker: *Gustav Stickley*
Date Made: *1900*
Dimensions: *24″ x 22″*
Value: *$6,000–9,000*

Experimental celandine tea table.

Some of the most sought-after furniture of the period was produced during Gustav's experimental years. Designs like the bungalow trestle table with its long keyed tenons and his series of small tables that incorporated Grueby pottery tiles on the tops are revered by even the most advanced collectors. The brief period Stickley spent producing these experimental pieces is evidence of how focused he was.

By 1900, Stickley's designs were beginning to develop into what he is primarily known for: furniture that is forceful, well built, and in keeping with his ideals. Even though machines had

The Gustav Stickley oval pull was introduced early in production and used through his remaining years.

been employed in the production of his furniture, the handwork was evident. It is not unusual to find tenons that vary on the same piece of furniture. Tenons protruding through the mortise were hand fitted, causing differences that were ever so slight. I have seen a number of examples where mortises were fitted with thin wedges to fill small gaps around tenons.

Stickley employed other details during these first years, including chamfered boards to form backs and panels on case pieces, flush tenons with crossed wedges and slightly

Strap hardware used on a mid-period Gustav Stickley sideboard.

chamfered edges, inverted-V supports, toe boards, and seat supports. He used the inverted-V, forming seat supports and toe boards on case pieces and as details on various other pieces.

Stickley hardware was finely hand wrought from copper, brass, or iron. Throughout the history of the Craftsman Workshops, all hardware was handmade. Each back plate was carefully hand-hammered and all of the cast parts were chased individually as if a piece of jewelry were being created. It is not unusual to see file marks on the heavy iron drawer pulls used on his earliest pieces. Even the iron escutcheon plates show handwork. Studying the evolution of Stickley's hardware, you will find many differences. His earliest pieces have hardware that is shaped and, on occasion, even mimics hardware you would expect to see on English Arts and Crafts pieces.

INLAID WRITING DESK
Maker: *Gustav Stickley/Harvey Ellis*
Date Made: *1903*
Dimensions: *29¼" x 29½" x 17"*
Value: *$60,000 +*

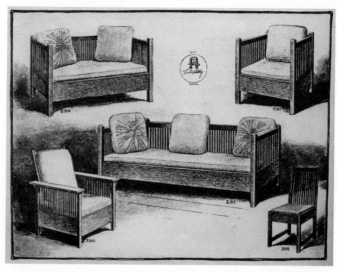

Catalog page showing a portion of Gustav Stickley's
spindle furniture line, ca 1907.

In 1903, Gustav hired the brilliant architect Harvey Ellis, who subsequently changed the direction of the Craftsman Workshops. Dying after less than a year with Gustav, Ellis had nonetheless produced some of the best work to come out of the Craftsman Workshops. He approached furniture design as an architect concentrating on form, not construction. Because his designs lack visible construction details, the best finishes are nearly black since they accentuate the forms. The black finishes also make the inlays of metal and wood Ellis used stand out. The best pieces of Ellis-designed furniture were produced while he was alive. As time passed, the designs were changed. Caned seat foundations were changed to spring seats; simple, elegant straps used as drawer pulls were replaced with V pulls; and finishes were lightened, interrupting the emphasis on form that darker finishes accentuated.

There is one thing I have to add here: the arch was not invented by Ellis. It has been used for thousands of years. He did, however, incorporate an exaggerated arch in his designs that is commonly referred to as the Ellis arch.

By the beginning of Gustav's "mature production" period, Gustav had things figured out. The different lines he produced made him successful. His furniture was structural and extremely well thought out. The machine began to play a greater role in his production and pieces began to display less handwork. I believe he was trying to reach a greater number of people. Employing the machine and dropping some of the handwork allowed him to reduce costs. Many of the designs he developed during the years from 1900 to 1904 were discontinued, however.

Spindle furniture introduced in 1905 may have been a response to the discontinued line of inlay furniture designed by Harvey Ellis. In the 1980s, spindle furniture was particularly hot; when a piece surfaced, it drew much attention. This attention has cooled off a bit, and this may be an area to consider collecting today. Great examples don't surface very often due to the rarity of spindle furniture. It's a line with much drama and works as well in a Prairie interior as in a Craftsman or bungalow interior because of its formal appearance. Finishes on the spindle line were normally a medium-dark color, rarely a black finish. Look for examples with straight spindles since the delicacy of the thin spindles often cause them to warp or twist.

As the period progressed, the competition became greater. Gustav responded to this competition by increasing production even more. This was the beginning of his "final mission" period. Many of his designs became lighter in scale and tended to be a bit less structural. Even with these production adjustments, his furniture was still better than the majority of his competitors. Gustav had a way with proportion. He seemed to follow a formula that allowed his designs to stand above the competition.

At the very end of Gustav's career with the Craftsman Workshops, he produced a line called Chromewald. He recognized that his empire was crumbling and needed a line that would help it survive. This line was also his response to the popularity of the Colonial Revival period. Chromewald, however, didn't work— and it still doesn't. This line was an interpretation of colonial design. Much of it was sold with a multicolored painted surface. Just because a piece has the joiner's compass company mark doesn't make it important or even collectable.

L. and J. G. Stickley handcraft decal used between 1906 and 1912.

The L. and J. G. Stickley Company

Two brothers, Leopold and John George Stickley, may have been the most successful furniture manufacturers of the twentieth century. Their company was one of the longest-surviving companies that began with the production of mission oak furniture. The firm's marketing and ability to change with the times was extraordinary. Leopold Stickley operated the company, which was established in 1902, until his death in 1957. His wife, Louise, then took over and ran the company until 1974. At that point, Alfred and Aminy Audi purchased the company that is now known as Stickley Audi and Company.

The company was located in Fayetteville, New York, only a short distance from their older brother Gustav's Craftsman Workshops. Their first company, known as Onondaga Cabinet Shops, named after the county in which Fayetteville is located, produced designs very similar to those of Gustav.

According to the extensive research of Michael Clark and Jill Thomas-Clark in their book *The Stickley Brothers: The Quest for an American Voice,* Leopold, at the beginning of his career, was caught in the shadows of his older brother Gustav. Starting in 1892, the two were connected in business. Examining the furniture Leopold began producing in 1902, it is evident that his designs were directly influenced by Gustav. This is when he opened his factory in Fayetteville and began producing furniture for other retailers, including Tobey Furniture Company and Paine Furniture. It wasn't until 1904 that Leopold and John George started advertising furniture on their own, publishing their first catalog promoting the Onondaga Shops, a line of furniture that in many cases resembled the furniture of Gustav.

L. and J. G. Stickley handcraft furniture catalog, ca 1905.

L. and J. G.'s first furniture lacked a refinement found later in their work. It had a crudeness to it. It was evident that they cut corners, probably in order to keep production costs down. For example, the curved horizontal back stretchers of chair backs were occasionally cut from solid boards instead of steam bent, and the arms of armchairs and rockers were held with wood screws and plugged. Also, the tenons and keys found on their bookcases were applied, something they continued throughout production. One detail that always surprised me were the applied tenons on the tops of the arms as if the tenons went straight through. This shortcut may have also been unacceptable at the time since the applied tenons were replaced with a true mortis and tenon by the handcraft period.

The Onondaga Shops period was one of experimentation and development. This and the handcraft period are my favorites. It is evident that the brothers were working through production and design problems. The earliest bookcases had nice, heavy mullions and a gallery back that was an inch and a half taller than their later cases, adding the same to the overall height. The wood used on the sides was thicker and often quartersawn oak was used throughout the piece. Also during this period, they tended to dowel every major joint, a practice they later dropped.

MAGAZINE STAND
Maker: *L. and J. G. Stickley*
Date Made: *1910*
Dimensions: *42" x 19¼" x 12"*
Value: *$2,500–3,500*

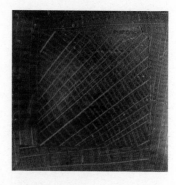

The unique quadrilinear post construction L. and J. G. Stickley used to produce their legs for tables, chairs, and settles.

I had the opportunity to compare, side by side, three number 46 magazine stands. The earliest (cataloged as number 346) was doweled at each intersection of wood. All the shelves and the toe board held securely. The next, a piece with a Handcraft decal, lacked the doweling to hold the center two shelves in place. The third, with a branded mark, the Work of L. and J. G. Stickley, was void of all dowels. The Onondaga piece had a real made-by-hand feel to it, and the last was most definitely a manufactured piece.

Leopold did develop advanced construction methods. The quatralinear post was used for strength and to display quarter-sawn wood on all four sides. The only problem with this today occurs when the wood separates. It is very difficult to restore. The company also used less veneer than other manufacturers, producing solid paneled doors and paneled cabinet ends.

When L. and J. G. furniture is good, it is very good and even great in the case of their line of Prairie-style furniture. The paneled and spindled Prairie arm chairs and settles are some of the most important designs produced during this period.

Leopold had developed a means of ensuring consistent finishing and design quality. Of course some designs are better than others, but the majority of their designs work together. L. and J. G.'s twenty-four-inch-diameter lamp tables, the examples with skirts under the tops and full shelves held by the lower stretchers, are better than their similar lightweight tables without skirts and a disk of oak floating on top of the stretchers.

CLOCK

Maker: *L. and J. G. Stickley*

Date Made: *1910*

Dimensions: *80½" x 21½" x 13"*

Value: *$60,000 +*

The tall case clock, catalog number 86, and the shelf clock, catalog number 85, are two of the best clocks from the period. The majestic height of the tall clock with the graduated size of the tenons and the subtle arches give it a formal power not found in other Arts and Crafts clocks from the period. The mantel clock, with its tapering body and broad overhanging top and base, works as well in a bungalow as in a Prairie setting. These two pieces could be included in even the best Arts and Crafts furniture collections.

The bottom line when collecting pieces from these second- and third-tier furniture companies is condition. L. and J. G. Stickley's yield was great in relative terms. The later during the period an item was produced, the less rare it usually is. Of course this is a generalization, but it should be kept in mind.

Roycroft Shops

The Roycroft Shops lasted forty-three years. Established by Elbert Hubbard in 1895, the company went bankrupt in 1938. Surprisingly, the furniture they produced was an afterthought, filler for builders completing an expansion of the very successful bookshop. David Cathers, a well-known author and researcher, quotes an excerpt from Hubbard's *Little Journey to the Homes of the Great* where Hubbard wrote:

Roycroft mark cut into solid oak 2⅛" tall.

> The place got too small when we began to bind books so we built a wing on one side; then a wing on the other. To keep three carpenters busy who had built the wings, I set them to work making furniture for the place. They made it as good as they could—folks came along and bought it.

Mr. Cathers pointed out that this took place in 1896 and 1897. Hubbard had neither a furniture background nor a design background, so one would only suspect that his earliest designs were born of necessity. The simplicity of his furniture is considered by some the root of mission furniture in America.

Roycroft furniture can be described as massive, austere, and direct. It has a form-follows-function look about it. The Roycroft Shops produced some outstanding furniture designs and some questionable designs as well. They had a tendency to play off of late Victorian designs, particularly evident in the shape of the arms on some of their Morris chairs and the bases to some of their tables. This is not necessarily a bad thing; it's just that it works on some pieces and not on others. In *A Catalog of Roycroft Furniture and Other Things,* dated 1906, Elbert Hubbard said, "We would ask you not to class our products as 'Mission,' or so called 'Mission Furniture.' Ours is purely Roycroft-made by us according to our own ideas." Puritanical, head-strong statements like this can be found throughout Hubbard's writings. This attitude seems to have been transferred to Roycroft's furniture designs as well.

Roycroft furniture construction tended to be that of a simple mortise and tenon, keyed or not, and held in place by a dowel pin. Another detail used on many Roycroft designs was a tapered leg ending in a bulbous foot. This is referred to as a Mackmurdo foot, after the British architect and designer Arthur Mackmurdo. One of the easiest ways to

No. 028. Arm Chair
25 inches wide,   22 inches deep,   38 inches high
Leather Seat
Oak, $15.00   Mahogany, $18.00

Roycroft Furniture catalog published after 1915.

DRESSER WITH MIRROR

Maker: *Roycroft Shops*

Date Made: *1915*

Dimensions: *61½" x 43½" x 25½"*

Value: *$7,000–10,000*

A page from the Roycroft furniture catalog dated 1908.

recognize a piece of Roycroft furniture is by the signature. Nearly all of Hubbard's furniture had a large and obvious orb mark and/or the word *Roycroft* in script. One of the most common pieces was a bookstand known as *A Little Journeys Stand,* which allegedly was a giveaway when customers purchased a set of Hubbard's *Little Journey* books. Even this piece was marked with a small copper tag affixed in a somewhat obvious place.

Roycroft furniture can be found in a variety of woods, including quartersawn white oak, ash, and mahogany. Many colors of oak were offered, including dark, medium, and light, as well as Roycroft brown, Flemish, golden, and Japanese gray. The amount of Roycroft furniture made from mahogany that surfaces today proves how popular it was among Hubbard's followers. The company offered dark, medium, and light mahogany pieces. In ash, they offered brown, Japanese gray, and silver gray.

The company's finishing process was, to a certain extent, unique. They first applied a stain made from rusty water mixed with stain and then applied a finish coat of wood filler and wax. Their finishes were quite vulnerable to anything that came in contact with them. I believe they recognized this and sometime during their production introduced a more typical shellac finish, which was applied thinly and then waxed. Because of this unique

PEDESTAL BOOKCASE
Maker: *Roycroft*
Date Made: *1910*
Dimensions: *64" x 22½" x 18"*
Value: *$12,000–18,000*

staining and finishing process, colors are deep and rich — the darker the finish, the better. These heavy forms lose something in a light finish. Wear is acceptable and in some cases enhances the look of the piece. A black-brown finish with some warm highlights can be quite beautiful.

Roycroft furniture production was small compared to other companies' production. Variations on different forms are not uncommon. Sometimes these work and sometimes they look like afterthoughts. The pieces with the name "Roycroft" spelled out are the most desirable (if it's in script, it's even better). Some of the better forms are their catalog number 085 three-door bookcases, the number 080 tall magazine pedestal, the number 050 mouse hole tabouret, and the number 055 chafing dish cabinet, to name a few. The number 0105 bedstead along with a number of their dining chairs are among their weaker designs. There is a formula to figure the relationship between the height of the back and the size and spacing of the slats in chairs that make for an appealing design, and many times the Roycroft Shops didn't get it. When they did, as in the number 033 hall chair, the piece was brilliant. Even the number 031 hall chair works.

Limbert Arts and Crafts Furniture

Charles Limbert did some outstanding work and was one of the pioneer furniture makers of the Arts and Crafts period. Limbert's line of Dutch Arts and Crafts furniture introduced in 1902 was heavy-handed massive furniture that emphasized weight of form and visible true construction techniques.

Branded mark used by Charles P. Limbert Company after 1904.

A 1¼" Limbert square drawer pull used on a Limbert library table.

This furniture was produced from ash the majority of the time, although oak was also used. It is quite possible that Charles Limbert felt that this heavy ash furniture was compatible with the Old Hickory log furniture from Martinsville, Indiana, which he sold and helped popularize. Limbert wrote that his designs for this earliest line shared a relationship with Dutch designs from as early as the fifteenth century. Indeed, Limbert's massive furniture, with its obviously handcrafted qualities, shows Dutch influence.

The hardware Limbert used also had a hand-wrought quality to it, a crudeness that blended perfectly with the wide-open grain of the ash and the massive proportions used. His earliest hardware was quite simple. It had a shaped back plate of steel or copper with an uncomplicated ring bail of like material that was simply attached or hardware that was fashioned from the same wood as the case. Later, the hardware became more sophisticated, produced of cast bronze or brass with back plates of solid copper that were bent, formed, shaped, and pierced until they blended nicely with the furniture.

Showing his energetic marketing skills, Limbert keyed in on the local populace, which happened to be of Scandinavian descent. Was it by coincidence that he opened a company in Holland, Michigan? His design department was fully aware of designs being produced in Europe. Limbert, prior to 1900, had in his employ a designer named Lewis Gohlke, about whom little is known. In 1903, Gohlke's son William also came to work for Charles

CAFE CHAIR
Maker: *Charles Limbert*
Date Made: *1910*
Dimensions: *34 ½" x 25 ½" x 21 ¼"*
Price: *$7,000–12,000*

Limbert and was responsible for catalog layout and many of the graphics used in Limbert's advertising. He may also have had a hand in furniture design.

Many of the Limbert pieces show Viennese and Glasgow influence. By 1905, Limbert had a line of furniture with square cutouts that could be compared to the work of Scottish designer Charles Rennie Mackintosh or well-known Viennese designer Joseph Hoffman.

A full line of finishes was offered. The choices were described in the catalog: "Genuine Fumed, Flanders, Holland Oak, Weathered, Early English, Stratford Oak, Golden Oak, Waxed, etc., or stained to match interior woodwork or to harmonize with decorations or furnished unfinished in the white."

These pieces were constructed using blind and visible splines as the primary method of joinery, allowing the forms to stand on their own without any embellishment. This also permitted the construction of sheets of solid wood, which allowed the designer to easily cut shapes from this solid sheet. Other companies that didn't use this process created their designs using more traditional methods. Dark finishes on these pieces are best because they accentuate the form and negative space the cutouts created. This square cutout furniture is considered the company's best.

The cafe chair, a knockoff of a McIntosh design, is great and works best with a dark finish. I also like their small tapering bookcase with shelves traveling up the sides. The single-door version is best, although the double-door version is very charming.

A page from the Limbert catalog showing a portion of their line incorporating square cutouts.

This square cutout line consisted of mostly seating, table, and case pieces, such as bookcases and desks. The values of these pieces have increased dramatically, and I suspect this trend will continue, particularly in the case of rarer examples. This may have been Limbert's most innovative work but not necessarily his most popular during the period. These pieces, however, are the most sought after by today's collectors, as evidenced by the amount of material that circulates through the marketplace now and the premium prices collectors are willing to pay for specimens in top condition.

ARM CHAIR WITH EBONY INLAY
Maker: *Charles Limbert*
Date Made: *1915*
Dimensions: *41" x 28" x 25½"*
Value: *$4,000–6,000*

BOOKCASE WITH INLAY
Maker: *Charles Limbert*
Date Made: *1905*
Dimensions: *50" x 63" x 15½"*
Value: *$15,000–25,000*

Even as late as 1915, Limbert developed another line called Ebon-oak. This line featured conservatively proportioned pieces with a simple inlay of ebony squares connected by a thin line of the same material. The finish color on these pieces, in contrast to the cutout line, comes across best in a medium- or light-colored finish that allows the inlay to stand out. Again, due to the number of Ebon-oak pieces that have surfaced, the production of this line may have been limited.

By this time, there were many companies across the country producing large quantities of furniture in the mission style that sold for less. This mass of furniture that hit the market was detrimental to the few companies that produced a quality product. This, combined with the expense of producing a line with inlay, may explain its rarity. When we think of Arts and Crafts furniture with inlay, Harvey Ellis immediately comes to mind. However, Limbert also produced a line with metal inlays and vignettes of scenic marquetry as surface decoration to enhance furniture. This furniture was primarily a close copy of Ellis's designs, with a few exceptions. Charles Limbert's inlaid furniture was a very limited line consisting of only a few different forms. Perhaps due to the cost of production, this furniture was very short-lived.

CHINA CABINET SHOWING CONSTRUCTION
Maker: *Charles Limbert*
Date Made: *1912*
Dimensions: *55¼" x 30½" x 14¼"*
Value: *$4,000–6,000*

Limbert's primary product was conservative, simple mission-style furniture. The proportion and weight was anything but severe. For the most part, it was well made using the typical mortise-and-tenon construction with exposed tenons where appropriate.

The *Limbert Arts and Crafts Furniture* catalog, booklet number 112, stated, "We use solid White Oak exclusively in the manufacture of our Holland Dutch Arts and Crafts furniture." Most of the other companies producing furniture during the height of this period offered furniture in maple and mahogany as well. The hardware was a mass-produced variety of cast brass or bronze, finished nicely but showing little, if any, handwork. This was produced by the Grand Rapids Brass Company, which supplied hardware for a number of Grand Rapids manufacturers. The majority of these furniture pieces had finish colors in the medium to light finish range. I suspect these finishes were the most popular and thus easiest to sell.

The contemporary market for this furniture is reasonably strong, and the majority of forms are collected by people interested in furnishing in this style. The values of the pieces have increased steadily over the past thirty years but not as dramatically as the other rarer cutout, Ebon-oak, or inlaid lines of furniture.

Stickley Brothers Company

The legacy left by the Stickley family was an appreciation of a simple, joyful lifestyle set against a backdrop of beautiful surroundings. Albert, a younger brother of Gustav, was also responsible for the Stickley legacy. Albert and brother J. George began their operations in Grand Rapids in 1892. Albert was a very enterprising businessman. His company produced a variety of styles and stayed in tune with the needs and trends of the time both in America and abroad.

Albert's aggressive business nature launched his company onto the international scene. By 1897, Stickley Brothers opened a factory in England with showrooms in London. Many of their earliest furniture designs fell into the category of Art Nouveau. Because of this connection with England, they were also producing furniture in the English Arts and Crafts vocabulary as well. This design trend seemed to stick with them well into the period.

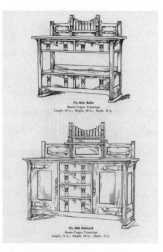

Catalog page showing English-inspired pieces with decorative copper. Date unknown.

Looking through their catalogs, you find pieces with complicated backboards, stained glass, and copper repoussé insets as well as large strap hinges with repoussé hearts and spades. These pieces were influenced by Liberty of London designs and other English designers and manufacturers.

This period between 1900 and 1905 may have been Stickley Brothers' best; it was definitely the most imaginative. Aggressive designs such as plank back chairs with inlay and furniture with decorative copper used as ornamental construction elements were unlike furniture produced by other Grand Rapids companies. This earlier period inspires the most interest among collectors today.

The Grand Rapids location was probably doing very well at this time, though they closed their England location in 1902. The brothers still remained high on the list of successful companies. This is evident by the amount of their furniture that shows up in today's market.

One thing for certain is that Stickley Brothers produced a quality product. Their wood choice was prime, their joinery true, and their finishing top shelf. Grand Rapids was near the heart of logging country in Michigan and Stickley Brothers took advantage of this. The white oak chosen for their furniture was some of the best to be found. It is a rare occasion to find a piece of Stickley Brothers furniture made of a plain sawn piece of wood used inappropriately.

When it was possible to make the construction visible, they took advantage of this situation, also. Mortise and tenon, splines, and dowels were all part of their production. They weren't afraid of letting their customers know that they employed machinery in their furniture production. The mortise and tenons used on some of their pieces were rounded on the top and bottom, showing the obvious lack of hand fitting, which was not necessarily a bad thing. Analyze the size and shape of the splines used to join two boards together to identify an unmarked piece.

Unlike other companies, Albert had little to say in his catalogs regarding his finishing process. Where others would go to great

CHINA CABINET

Maker: *Stickley Brothers*

Date Made: *1905*

Dimensions: *59" x 48" x 17"*

Value: *$6,000–9,000*

China cabinet with decorative copper.

lengths to describe the process they followed and the colors they offered, the Stickley Brothers catalogs simply stated, "All Oak furniture finished in Fumed Oak or any other finish desired." This showed the latitude of their finishing room and their philosophy that the customer is always right. The majority of pieces that I have seen on the market are medium to medium light in color, which may have been easier for them to sell. During the height of the production of mission oak, the scale of their pieces were on the lighter side, and this may also have contributed to their decision to finish their product in a lighter color.

In today's market, Stickley Brothers furniture has the widest appeal to people interested in furnishing a home with less-expensive quality pieces produced during the period. Stickley Brothers furniture is an excellent product that has held its value over the years. Their mid-period furniture was nicely proportioned, lighter in scale, and displayed excellent construction, finishing techniques, and hardware. Even the best of Stickley Brothers pieces can be found at a relatively moderate price.

Stickley Brothers produced several lines that have decorative value only, including furniture produced with rope-turned legs and painted cottage sets. Neither of these lines, although reminiscent of their Arts and Crafts furniture, has much to do with the period. These were produced later in the century and cross into the Colonial Revival period.

A Plan for Collecting

The Arts and Crafts period is more than a collecting phenomenon —it's a lifestyle. One of the attractions of this period is its philosophy of simplicity. People start collecting Arts and Crafts furniture for many different reasons. Some people are interested in the historical importance of the period; some merely want to furnish a newly purchased bungalow. Whether you're just beginning or have been collecting for a while, you should develop a plan. Every household has specific needs. William Morris said, "Have nothing in your houses that you do not know to be useful or believe to be beautiful."

It is important to do your homework, know what is available, what the values are, and where to get what you want. Be informed. Building a library of reference material is the best place to start. Being able to reference what you are looking at will make the whole collecting process more enjoyable.

You should consider proportion and scale in order to achieve a flow in your collection. For example, placing a Gustav Stickley V-back rocker next to a Gustav drop-arm Morris will look odd because of the size difference. However, a Limbert oversized rocker may be perfect. Make the forms work together. Pieces should be proportionate to your space. I wouldn't be concerned with differences in finish colors; mixing up finishes will add interest.

Your collection could be focused on one maker or it could be eclectic. I've seen both approaches and either can work. Many companies offered a line of a certain design — for example, Limbert's square cutout furniture line or the Lifetime Company's Puritan line. My advice is to buy the best you can afford regardless of the maker. You will always appreciate the pieces more in the end. As you collect, your eye will mature. Follow your gut feeling, and don't be afraid to trade up.

Sooner or later, the issue of condition will arise — that is, original versus restored. Sometimes, in order to obtain a form that you want, you will have to compromise. Replacing a refinished piece down the road is not unheard of. It has been said that "the time to buy an antique is when you see it." If you locate a form you've been looking for or come across a piece that intrigues you, but the condition is less than you would normally accept, don't pass on it immediately. Consider buying it while keeping the cost of restoration and upholstery in mind. If the piece warrants a professional evaluation, hire your restorer or dealer to inspect it for you. Knowing what's involved in the restoration process is very important and will help in evaluating furniture.

The criteria for our collecting is twofold: first, we want to live with things that are aesthetically pleasing and useful; second, we want to know that our collections will hold their value or increase in value over the years. The most important thing to remember is to do your homework and have fun collecting.

Arts and Crafts Lighting

MENTION LIGHTING DESIGN OF THE PERIOD TO ANY SERIOUS ARTS AND CRAFTS ENTHUSIAST and you'll likely get a laugh. It's difficult to reconcile our current notions about domestic light with those of a time when the common household bulb — for houses urban enough to have electricity — topped off at a whopping fifteen watts. Needless to say, if creating an absolutely authentic Arts and Crafts interior is what you're striving for, you may have to trade certain activities like reading after dark.

Maker: *Gustav Stickley*
Date Made: *ca 1902–1916*
Dimensions: *base 15"*
Value: *$8,000–12,000*

Gustav Stickley hammered copper oil lamp model number 376. There were multiple shade choices for each of these bases; the majority we see tend to be wicker as shown here.

Lighting created during this period is representative of the pace of changing technology that prevailed after the Industrial Revolution. The turn of the century was charged with new inventions. However, until at least 1920, the quickly evolving application of electricity in the home depended largely on geographical location — more people living in cities had electric lighting than people living in rural areas.

Electric lighting existed concurrently with earlier lighting methods, such as oil- or alcohol-filled lanterns, gas fixtures, and even candles. It's interesting to note the number

Maker: *Gustav Stickley*
Date Made: *ca 1902–1916*
Dimensions: *base 15"*
Value: *$6,000–8,000*

Gustav Stickley's hammered copper table lamp model number 295. Both this lamp and the hammered copper oil lamp on the left were wired for electricity, but both were originally oil fixtures. These designs incorporated reservoirs to hold fuel. The wick and flame were contained within a glass chimney.

of period interiors documented either as sketches or photographs that have electrified sconces and pendant fixtures in the same room with tabletop oil lamps. Wall outlets, a new technology at the turn of the century, were few and far between, thus making portable and cordless oil lamps the natural choice for work spaces or tabletops centrally located in a room. Within this context, it's easy to understand why period catalogs, like those of Gustav

Stickley, offer a wide array of designs for electric and fuel-powered fixtures and lamps. And why, from time to time, we encounter fuel-powered lamps that have been drilled for electrical cords and refitted with sockets (with varying degrees of expertise).

Much like the pottery, furniture, and metalwork of the period, the best lighting resonates with the creative force of its maker. No attempt was made to mask the evidence of the creative process; rather, the finished form celebrates its hand-wrought status with visible evidence of the maker's hand. Dovetail seams are visible on copper table lamps, patinas highlight raised surfaces, rivets and hammer marks are integral parts of the design, and the "imperfections" in hand-blown glass are readily apparent to the eye. While visiting the home of one prominent California collector of Dirk Van Erp lamps, I noticed that each lamp was turned so that the seams, which are always on the back, or cord

Detail of a hand-hammered Dirk Van Erp table lamp. Note the way the reddish brown patina highlights the planished copper and the rivets used to join the font to the base.

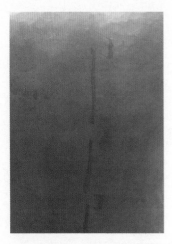

Detail of a hand-joined seam. The color difference in the dovetailing is not a flaw; rather, it is indicative of the silver solder against the copper.

side, and hence usually turned toward the wall, proudly faced out into the room.

Lighting that embodies an aesthetic driven by organic design has attracted the most attention from scholars and collectors. *Organic* is a complex term. On one level, it refers to a form that looks like something from the natural world. Who doesn't think of a mushroom cap when first viewing the glowing mica dome of a Dirk Van Erp lamp, or the bumpy, colorful skin of a harvest-time gourd when looking at the copper sheeting manipulated by Van Erp into one of his red, warty masterpieces? But *organic* also defines a systemic approach to design that is apparent in cohesive interiors of the period. While perhaps less literally organic in form than the lighting of studio artisans like Dirk Van Erp or Albert Berry, designs by the likes of Gustav Stickley and the Roycrofters are equally important as forms that we view as successful and immensely collectible today.

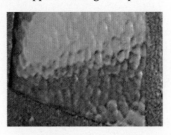

The pebbled texture of this amber glass comes from hammering it while it was hot with a ball peen. Bubbles in this type of glass are common and should not be considered flaws.

Maker: *Grueby/Bigelow and Kennard*
Date Made: *ca 1910*
Dimensions: *23"*
Value: *$35,000–45,000*

This Grueby base is topped with a leaded shade by Bigelow and Kennard.
While the pine cone design is unusual, more desirable are Grueby/Tiffany
collaborations.

Gustav Stickley

The 1901 Pan-American Exposition held in Buffalo was a combined exhibition of Gustav Stickley's United Crafts and the pottery of Grueby Faience Company.[1] (See page 273 for lighting chapter sources.) Stickley had been using Grueby tiles in his small table designs and the pairing was a natural one. Featured prominently in the center of an extant photograph is a large Grueby oil lamp base with a leaded-glass shade. Stickley reportedly believed Grueby pots to be the ideal accessories for harmonizing with his own furniture, and the ceramic bases were excellent vessels to contain the font necessary for a functioning oil lamp.[2] Lamps like the one in the photograph on the left appear in *Chips from the Craftsman Workshops* catalog and throughout the early retail plates and catalogs. The combined appeal of the Grueby pottery base with a period shade makes them immensely desirable today—electrified or not.

For Gustav Stickley, designing and making lighting within United Crafts was a first step in promoting his cohesive vision of the ideal home and in growing his business. Even his earliest furniture designs required hardware (hinges, pulls, escutcheons, and the like) of a very specific ilk to please his aesthetic, but nothing of the sort was readily available. There is continued debate over whether the Onondaga Metal Shops (which later became Benedict Studios) produced Gustav Stickley's early metalware, but it is clear from promotional material that

Maker: *Grueby/Tiffany*
Date Made: *ca 1910*
Dimensions: 22″
Value: *$20,000—30,000*

by 1902, Gustav Stickley's enterprise included a foundry that produced the hardware required to finish his furniture appropriately and the lighting and other decorative accessories he deemed fit to complement his interior designs. Interestingly, retail plates after 1904 feature exclusively Gustav Stickley's own

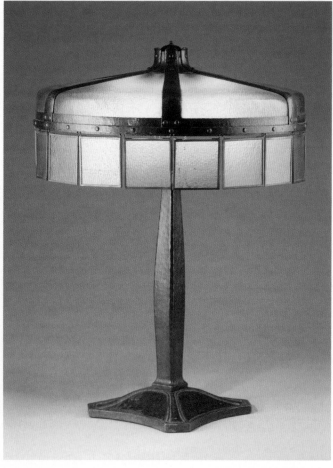

Maker: *Gustav Stickley*
Date Made: *ca 1902 –1916*
Dimensions: *35 ½"*
Value: *50,000–70,000*

Gustav Stickley's monumental table lamp model number 755. With a six-socket cluster, this lamp was clearly meant to illuminate libraries or offices of grander scale than the average bungalow.

lamp designs (though pottery props still appear to be Grueby, or Grueby-style, pieces).

Of his table lamps, the most impressive by far is the massive model number 755. The shade features curved, hammered amber glass and is hung with small copper-edged squares around the full diameter — presumably to filter the glare, for at the height of thirty-five inches, with a six-socket cluster, this lamp cast a large amount of light. Or perhaps the squares were used to economize and retrofit parts used in the copper and glass chandelier that was one of his earlier designs for use as a table lamp. The scale, combined with the cost (it bears a list price of

Maker: *Gustav Stickley*
Date Made: *ca 1902–1916*
Dimensions: *base 13 ½"*
Value: *$3,000–3,500*

Gustav Stickley's table lamp model number 56 ½ has a flaring base and was available in two sizes. This is the larger of the two.

Maker: *Gustav Stickley*
Date Made: *ca 1902–1916*
Dimensions: *base 9"*
Value: *$1,500–2,500*

Model number 503 bears a wicker shade like that of the 56 ½, but the oak base is more common than those found in hammered copper.

Maker: *Gustav Stickley*
Date Made: *ca 1902–1916*
Dimensions: *lantern 8" tall*
Value: *$1,000–1,500*

A Gustav Stickley lantern number 205 with spade cutouts in iron.

$115.00 while other table lamp styles top off at $20!), must have made this a difficult purchase for the average homeowner, but it is a prized form today.

Electroliers and sconces, bearing cutouts we now call hearts but were initially meant as stylized, spade-shaped leaves, I believe, are the fixtures we see most commonly. No small wonder that these were clearly very popular designs that were offered in no less than nine different variations, from single pendants to a nine-lantern chandelier in the 1905 catalog of hand-wrought metal.[3] The spade cutout lanterns and chandeliers were made in hand-wrought iron, hammered copper, and brass, though the examples we see are rarely brass. Of the iron and copper fixtures, there is definitely a preference among collectors for the finer look of hammered copper.

More rare are the elegant hanging pendants inspired by, if not

Maker: *Gustav Stickley*
Date Made: *ca 1902–1916*
Dimensions: *lantern 8" tall;*
wall mount 5 ½" sq.
Value: *$3,500–4,500*

Though rarer than either the iron or hammered copper versions of this lantern, fixtures with the original brass patina are not necessarily more desirable.

Maker: *Gustav Stickley*
Date Made: *ca 1902–1916*
Dimensions: *lantern 8" tall; bracket 10" tall*
Value: *$2,000–2,500*

The elegance of the rich copper patina in combination with hand-hammered marks make the same lantern in copper more desirable.

Maker: *Gustav Stickley*
Date Made: *ca 1902–1916*
Dimensions: *lantern 8" tall; band 12" in diameter*
Value: *$15,000–20,000*

*One of the multiple variations
of electrolier fitted with spade
lanterns was this three-light
version.*

Maker: *Gustav Stickley*

Date Made: *ca 1902–1916*

Dimensions: *lantern 8" tall; band 16" in diameter*

Value: *$25,000–35,000*

*A Gustav Stickley spade cutout electrolier with five lights.
The adjacent photo of a fixture made by Onondaga Metal Shops
illustrates design similarities that lend support to the idea that
there was an affiliation between the two shops.*

Maker: *Gustav Stickley*
Date Made: *ca 1902–1916*
Dimensions: *lantern 9" tall*
Value: *$3,500–5,000*

Maker: *Gustav Stickley*
Date Made: *ca 1902–1916*
Dimensions: *approx. 14"*
Value: *$35,000–60,000*

Model numbers 202 and 204 respectively are also Gustav Stickley lanterns but have more elegant lines and were likely influenced by European designs.

actually designed by, Harvey Ellis. Other Stickley designs run the gamut from almost severely architectural to old-world cottage, but contained within the same 1905 metalwork catalog are several lanterns whose graceful rooflines and shaped strap work depart from those confines. Armatures with either gentle curves outward or edges that taper and straps that billow, unrestrained by rivets along the roofline, bear the visual lightness that were the product of Ellis's brief term with Stickley.

Perhaps one of the most functional designs of the Craftsman line is the standing floor lamp model number 500. The wooden base, exhibiting subtle hammered-copper fittings, was available in either mahogany or fumed oak. Stickley refers to this piece as a piano lamp.[4] Indeed, with its pivoting shade mount, the design is one of the few period lamps that is actually useful for close work or reading.

Maker: *Gustav Stickley*
Date Made: *ca 1902–1916*
Dimensions: *lantern 15" tall*
Value: *$4,000–6,000*

Maker: *Gustav Stickley*
Date Made: *ca 1902–1916*
Dimensions: *lantern 8"*
Value: *$4,000–6,000*

Gustav Stickley lanterns model numbers 324 and 830 respectively have straight lines and architectural rooflines.

It is important to note that when shade and base are intact, the lamp is far more desirable. However, original shades were made of delicate materials, either linen-lined silk, or silk-lined cane, that did not age well.

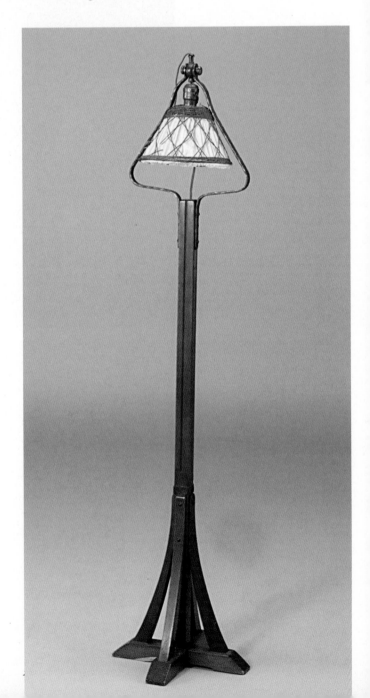

Stickley Brothers and Limbert

Stickley Brothers Company, though they get only a fraction of the attention of Gustav Stickley from collectors, also strived to provide a full line of accessories for their "Quaint" interiors. They began offering a line of Russian hand-beaten copper pieces as early as 1904.[5] Though equally compelled by the tradition of old-world crafts (for an interesting treatise on this subject see *The Collected Works of Gustav Stickley* by Stephen Gray), their

Maker: *Gustav Stickley*
Date Made: *ca 1902–1916*
Dimensions: *60" tall*
Value: *$3,000–3,500*

Gustav Stickley floor lamp model number 500 is shown here in mahogany with its original silk-lined wicker shade. The pivoting shade of this lamp makes it one of the more useful period forms for reading or close work.

Maker: *Gustav Stickley*
Date Made: *ca 1902–1912*
Dimensions: *approx. 22" tall*
Value: *$5,000–8,000*

A Stickley Brothers hand-hammered or beaten base topped by a corseted mica shade with a delicate hammered copper overlay.

Maker: *Stickley Brothers*
Date Made: *ca 1904–1912*
Dimensions: *approx. 22" tall*
Value: *$3,000–5,000*

Another Stickley Brothers table lamp of more diminutive scale than the previous example. Stickley Brothers table lamps are not uncommon but their best forms have proportioned elegant lines. Sconces and electroliers, like model numbers 353 and 300, are a departure from the American Arts & Crafts aesthetic and are quite rare.

metalware offerings, like their best furniture designs, display a marked departure from a purely American Arts and Crafts aesthetic. Documentation of their lighting is limited because we've yet to see many of these designs come to the market, but reprints of period catalogs display pages of lamps and fixtures that are clearly informed by more delicate British and Art Nouveau sensibilities and warrant more attention than they are currently afforded.

Interestingly, it is the Stickley Brothers metal shop that is credited with making lighting for Charles Limbert.[6] Limbert's designs bear shades overlaid with intricate cutouts in copper. Base styles range from elegantly corbelled fumed oak to hammered copper with finely worked straps. Ever interested in promoting the Dutch influence on American Arts and Crafts design, Limbert's most recognizable lamps have cutwork that is not

Maker: *Limbert/Stickley Brothers*
Date Made: *ca 1904–1912*
Dimensions: *24 ¼" tall*
Value: *$12,000–18,000*

The cutout shade of Limbert's windmill lamp is the whimsical rendering of a Dutch pastoral scene with a cat and female form in the foreground. The base itself represents the mill—note the "windows" ascending around the base as they would to illuminate the spiral staircase within a functioning mill.

Maker: *Limbert/Stickley Brothers*
Date Made: *ca 1904–1912*
Dimensions: *24 ½" tall*
Value: *$12,000–18,000*

Another Limbert design depicts a barge being pulled along a canal. Trees are in the foreground.

abstract or architectural like his most interesting furniture designs, but rather, displays whimsical renderings of windmills and ships under full sail.[7]

For those who find the windmills and goats *too* whimsical, there are lovely shades overlaid with stylized trees and foliage — though I should point out that the cutwork on model number 7 is recognizable to gardeners as a vine called Dutchman's Pipe.[8]

Roycroft Shops

The best lamps put forth by the Roycroft Shops were masterful designs in stained glass and oak by Dard Hunter. Hunter's first stint on the Roycroft campus began in 1903. Several versions of the simple leaded square patterns that have come to symbolize his work occupied the Roycroft Inn and Elbert Hubbard's office.[9] After returning to Roycroft from Vienna in 1909, Hunter collaborated briefly with Karl Kipp (they had both departed by 1911) in a newly expanded and organized metal shop.[10] Some of Roycroft's most inspired lighting designs emerged during this period. The marriage of graphic designs in glass and fine metalwork make these the most desirable Roycroft lamps and fixtures.

Other Roycroft lamps are also highly collectible. The talented

Maker: *Roycroft Shops*
Date Made: *ca 1920*
Dimensions: *24" tall*
Value: *$15,000–20,000*

A fine leaded-glass and hammered-copper table lamp designed by Dard Hunter. The simple, geometric pattern is complemented by the fiery highlights in the glass that emerge when it is illuminated.

Maker: *Roycroft Shops*
Date Made: *ca 1920*
Dimensions: *24" tall*
Value: *$20,000–30,000*

Though similar to the previous example, the more sophisticated lead pattern and subtle colors make this an exceptional example of Dard Hunter's designs.

artisans of the Roycroft metal shop were able to produce a varied number of stock forms. Copper table lamp styles with domed shades and mica inserts are highly coveted for their workmanship and design, as are smaller boudoir lamps. Examples with the original glass shades are rare and sought after by collectors.

Maker: *Roycroft Shops*
Date Made: *ca 1915*
Dimensions: *approx. 15 ½" tall*
Value: *$1,500–2,500*

Smaller boudoir lamps like this one are fairly common and are often referred to as helmet lamps. Lack of glass parts likely helped these lamps survive intact.

Maker: *Roycroft Shops*
Date Made: *1920*
Dimensions: *approx. 14 ½" tall*
Value: *$7,500–9,500*

Original glass shades make this form rare and desirable.

Maker: *Roycroft Shops*
Date Made: *ca 1920*
Dimensions: *approx. 14 ½"*
Value: *$3,500–5,500*

Fine hammering, simple lines, and detailed strap work make this copper table lamp with celluloid inserts highly collectible.

Dirk Van Erp

The initial incarnation of Dirk Van Erp's metal studio opened in Oakland, California, in 1908. Aside from his skill as a copper-smith, what set Van Erp lighting apart from the aforementioned firms is that his studio focused completely on the production of quality hand-wrought copper items without concern for marketing or promoting a lifestyle. That said, he did operate a studio and was clearly interested in earning his living and supporting the employees required to maintain production.

Differences in the shop mark used by Van Erp to sign his wares along with various documented collaborations and partnerships have made it possible for scholars and collectors to separate his

Maker: *Dirk Van Erp*
Date Made: *ca 1910*
Dimensions: *approx. 14"*
Value: *$12,000–20,000*

The compelling proportions along with an unusual shade cap design make this small lamp a good example of Van Erp's collaboration with D'Arcy Gaw.

Maker: *Dirk Van Erp*
Date Made: *ca 1910*
Dimensions: *approx. 15"*
Value: *$10,000–15,000*

Another small table lamp from the Van Erp/Gaw era. Note the shape of the inset mica panel created by the joining of the strap to the shade cap.

work into marked periods of production. Of these, his partnership with designer and artisan D'Arcy Gaw gets the most attention. It is thought that lamps were not a part of Van Erp's repertoire until this partnership began in 1910, though a photo of the studio show-room circa 1909 clearly shows a lamp base among the offer-ings.[11] Regardless, the best designs that emerged from this brief period (the partnership with Gaw lasted less than a year) are sought after for their graceful lines, balanced proportion, and the early shop mark containing both names.

RIGHT: The original shop mark bearing the names of both D'Arcy Gaw and Dirk Van Erp. Ca 1910.

LEFT: The shadow of the name D'Arcy Gaw is still apparent after her name is struck from the die after only about a year of partnership.

RIGHT: Though D'Arcy Gaw's name is removed, the rest of the die is intact. This is a closed box mark. Approximate dates of this mark are 1911–1915.

LEFT: The right side of the box is no longer a part of the die. This is an open box mark and dates after approximately 1915. A second die "San Francisco" was used, likely because of the studio's involvement in an exposition.

RIGHT: The second die, "San Francisco," though not used on every piece, can appear within the box or near the box as on this piece.

After Gaw's departure, her name was removed from the shop mark. There is both supposition and lore about the terms of her departure, but the practical benefit of the separation was that this first alteration to the die stamp led to other visible changes as the result, thus giving us an interesting dateline for tracking design and construction changes in Van Erp pieces.

One way to categorize Van Erp lamps is by the engineering of their shades. The first designs had a single piece of copper seamed, hammered, and shaped to the appropriate cant and finish. They were then bordered with a rolled edge on the outer ring of the shade skeleton. In some pieces after about 1915, shade designs still have a rolled edge but also have a central crease in the band that resulted in a flat, linear fascia. Yet another variation is formed with the addition of a roll at the point where the

Van Erp shades with a single rolled rim were made throughout the life of the studio. The roll is formed by hand.

Maker: *Dirk Van Erp*
Date Made: *post-1915*
Dimensions: *approx. 15"*
Value: *$8,000–12,000*

Shades with a crease and a rolled rim appeared on lamp designs after about 1915.

Maker: *Dirk Van Erp*
Date Made: *ca 1915*
Dimensions: *18" tall*
Value: *$18,000–25,000*

Rarely seen and extremely collect-ible are shades with mica inserts around the rim like this one.

Maker: *Dirk Van Erp*
Date Made: *post-1915*
Dimensions: *approx. 18" tall*
Value: *$12,000–20,000*

*This double rolled rim, though made with the help of a rolling machine,
is difficult to execute. Note that the straps are riveted under the
shade cap — this design element is seen in shades after 1915.*

band is creased—the double rolled rim. The creases and rolls
were formed with the aid of a machine, and the piece of metal
was then seamed. The resulting lamps are powerful testaments
to skill and craftsmanship. However, premiums are placed on
lamps with a single rolled edge because they are thought, incor-
rectly, to have required more skill to make.[12]

Van Erp is especially known for pieces he chose not to finish with fine hammering marks. Known as "warty" because of the lumps in the copper left unplanished before they were patinated, these pieces exist in standard brown and irregular shades of red patina. It is reported that the red was Dirk Van Erp's favorite patina and that he kept its exact process a secret.[13] It is therefore highly coveted by collectors.

Maker: *Dirk Van Erp*
Date Made: *ca 1915*
Dimensions: *24 ½" tall*
Value: *$75,000–150,000 +*

Though rare, one of the most coveted of Van Erp's designs is the milk can. It is monumental in size and elegant in form.

Maker: *Dirk Van Erp*
Date Made: *post-1911*
Dimensions: *18 ½" tall*
Value: *$18,000–30,000*

This flat-topped table lamp was designed by Van Erp's nephew. It is appealing because of its graceful cutwork and unusual form.

Van Erp and his studio produced metalwork of the highest consistent quality. But his skills as an artist and coppersmith are most apparent in the items he chose to leave in their warty state. Allowing the maker's hand to show in each hand-wrought item was the Arts and Crafts ideal—and Van Erp challenged prevailing sensibilities even further by presenting pieces as beautiful in an even less manipulated form.

Lighting Sources

1. Coy L. Ludwig, *The Arts and Crafts Movement in New York State: 1890s–1920s* (Layton, UT: Gibbs Smith, Publisher, 1984), 56.

2. Ibid., 4.

3. Stephen Gray, *The Collected Works of Gustav Stickley* (Maplewood, NJ: Turn of the Century Editions, 1989), 153–171.

4. Stephen Gray, *The Early Works of Gustav Stickley* (Maplewood, NJ: Turn of the Century Editions, 1988), 157.

5. Don Marek, *Grand Rapids Art Metalwork 1902–1918* (Grand Rapids, MI: Heartwood, 1999), 52.

6. Stephen Gray, *Limbert Furniture* (Maplewood, NJ: Turn of the Century Editions, 1988), 6.

7. Marek, *Grand Rapids Art Metalwork 1902–1918,* 48.

8. Gray, *Limbert Furniture,* 9.

9. Robert Judson Clark, ed., *The Arts and Crafts Movement in America 1876–1916* (Princeton, NJ: Princeton UP, 1992), 46.

10. Bruce Johnson and David Rago, *The Official Identification and Price Guide to American Arts & Crafts,* 3rd ed. (New York: House of Collectables, 2003), 362.

11. Isak Lindenauer. *Wildflower,* Issue 1.

12. Ibid.

13. Dorothy Lamoureux, *The Arts and Crafts Studio of Dirk Van Erp* (San Francisco: Museum of Craft & Folk Art, 1989), 21.

Arts and Crafts Metalwork

THE WEIGHT, TEMPERATURE, AND STRENGTH OF A PIECE OF HAND-WROUGHT METAL all contribute to a singular, tactile experience, especially if it is expertly executed and perfectly balanced. Whether it's a set of nesting ashtrays by the Roycrofters or a monumental jardiniere by master metalsmith Dirk Van Erp, this can be a defining moment for an Arts and Crafts collector.

Unlike ceramics, collecting Arts and Crafts metal did not begin until the time of the Princeton Exhibition in 1972. We feel the metal market has always taken a back seat to the study of furniture and pottery. With fewer dedicated collectors, Arts and Crafts–period metal has mostly been treated as an accessory to furniture.

Metal is perceived by many as a masculine medium, one that took strength to manipulate. Dirk Van Erp, Karl Kipp, and Walter Jennings were a few of the accomplished men who created beautiful objects during the period. But the perception is false, as plenty of women were involved in producing some of the finest examples known. While we have chosen not to include women like Elizabeth Burton because she is best known for her lighting pieces, and the ladies of the Kalo Shops because they worked primarily in silver, women contributed to a body of work that was clearly defined and supported by both sexes.

One word of caution: though many of the best pieces of the period are marked at least by the manufacturer, if not the individual artist, we've seen some very convincing marks on fakes. We recall, around 1999, a number of phony Gustav Stickley pieces that came to market. Even though the die-stamped compass marks were nearly perfect, the objects themselves were clearly

VAN ERP VASE
Date Made: *ca 1905*
Dimensions: *12" tall*
Value: *$6,000–8,000*

*Dirk Van Erp hammered copper vase with a broad shoulder
and a rolled rim under a rich, dark brown patina.*

of a later vintage and of odd metals such as brass. The pieces lacked the grace and character that separate the fine originals from the later frauds.

Manufacturers

Perhaps one of the reasons there are fewer collectors of just period metal as opposed to ceramics or furniture is that there were relatively few masterpieces created. Most of the metalwork produced during the period were gift items or small accessories for the home, such as desk sets, bud vases, and candlesticks. For every Roycroft mixed-metal Secessionist vase, for example, there are probably 250 pairs of bookends. Though handmade, they were produced by the thousands and marketed nationwide. It is for this reason that fine metal shops such as Heintz, the Arts Crafts Shop, and the Minneapolis Guild are not included in this chapter.

Obviously, outstanding collections are comprised of outstanding pieces. We will limit our coverage to the producers of the most important period material available on the market today.

Roycroft Shops

The Roycroft Shops produced an enormous amount of art metal. The community was founded initially in 1895 to print fine books, and they did not begin hammering metal of any sort until about 1899. Even then, their work was of an experimental nature, providing their furniture shops with hardware in the slow pursuit of their own style. It wasn't until ten years later that their metal shop began actively producing art ware. It was about this time that they created much of their finest work.

The hammering of Roycroft metal is very controlled and precise, which is almost startling when you consider the consistent quality of their vast production. Earlier work is usually of a heavier gauge of copper, and an earlier cylinder vase will feel like a length of pipe. The later work, made after World War I, is usually much lighter in weight.

Roycroft also employed several patinas. A light brown, found on earlier pieces, may have resulted from the lack of a chemically

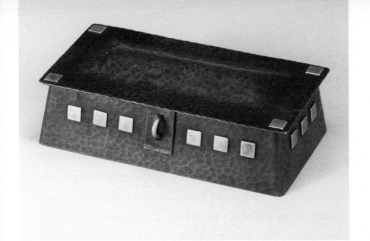

ROYCROFT JEWELRY BOX
Maker: *Design by Dard Hunter and Karl Kipp*
Date Made: *ca 1912*
Dimensions: *7" x 3"*
Value: *$10,000–15,000*

Exceptional Roycroft two-metal jewelry box design. German nickel squares on a wrought copper base. Original dark patina.

induced patina, allowing age to create the color. Aurora Brown, which is their most popular finish, is a rich, deep chocolate brown, chemically produced with a lacquered surface. Rarely, these pieces are enhanced with what Roycroft called an Italian Polychrome technique, where they rubbed green pigment into some of the stippled design areas.

Roycroft also used surfaces other than copper. Old Brass, for example, is a brass plating

ROYCROFT SHAFT VASE
Date Made: *ca 1915*
Dimensions: *10" tall*
Value: *$3,500–4,500*

Early Roycroft cylinder vase with flaring base and riveted foot under a rich, dark patina.

over copper. Blue Brass is also a brass plating over copper, but has a blue iridescent gunmetal effect. In limited production was their Sheffield finish, a silver-over-copper plating, occasionally with an acid-etched surface. While there are always exceptions, their best work is typically found with a brown patina on copper.

You should look for earlier pieces, made prior to World War I, that are heavy, brown, and bear the early company logo. Even better are those designed by Karl Kipp and Dard Hunter, with German silver added as a second metal. The least of these two metal pieces count among their better work, and the best of them are just short of genius. Work by Walter Jennings is prized for the tooled designs he added to the wrought finishes. Victor Toothacher, who would eventually leave Hubbard and go to work for Gustav Stickley, is credited with designing one of the more popular vases, the Grove Park Inn American Beauty Vase. Toothacher was also responsible for a few of the better lighting designs. Each of these artists brought individuality and a creative distinctiveness to the copper shop.

Later pieces of Roycroft, those made after about 1925, were produced long after the Arts and Crafts period was over. These are often simply stamped from sheet metal, show little handiwork, and exhibit overall poor design. They usually bear a Roycroft mark that is similar to the early designation, but there is no ball at the end of the R's right leg, and the spelled-out word *Roycroft* is often added. Many of these later pieces have an acid-

ROYCROFT VASE
Maker: *Design by Walter Jennings*
Date Made: *ca 1915*
Dimensions: *4" tall*
Value: *$2,000–2,500*

Early Roycroft cylinder vase of heavy gauge metal with original dark patina over a tooled floral design.

etched surface. This was a technique mostly employed during the end of their run because it took a fraction of the time to score a surface with chemicals than it did for a craftsman to hammer the surface. If you're looking only for the firm's best work, avoid them.

Pieces should be in near-original condition, with good, even patinas showing little wear or scarring. Obviously, if you have the chance to buy a rare masterpiece, you should be willing to accept an appropriate amount of wear. The important thing to remember about the Roycrofters is that, while the bulk of their production centered on catalog ware, their best artists were able to ad-lib pieces from time to time. Look for such examples.

Gustav Stickley

Gustav Stickley's Craftsman Workshops' output of metalwork was relatively small in comparison with that of their cross-state competitors, the Roycrofters. The limited quantity of unique Stickley designs attests to this. Their pieces tend to be simple

STICKLEY DESK SET
Maker: *Craftsman Workshops*
Date Made: *ca 1910*
Dimensions: *blotter desk is 15" x 25"*
Value: *$5,000–7,500*

Gustav Stickley desk set made of heavy gauge copper with original dark patina.

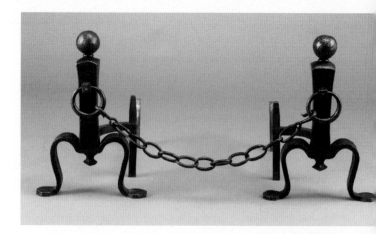

STICKLEY ANDIRONS
Maker: *Craftsman Workshops*
Date Made: *ca 1905*
Dimensions: *20" tall*
Value: *$5,000–7,000*

Gustav Stickley wrought iron andirons with original connecting chain under a black finish.

designs that are meant to accompany the furniture Stickley created. Nevertheless, pieces bearing the Craftsman joiner's compass logo are uniformly fine. The problem is that little of this work was truly exceptional.

Stickley's work was of heavy gauge copper with rich, dark patinas. While there was some variation in color, we do not see the disparity in finishes that were used at Roycroft. Of particular import are larger vases, andiron and fireplace sets, decorated chargers or plaques, and coal scuttles or handled buckets.

It is important to remember that there was a great deal of competition between other neighboring companies such as the Onondaga Metal Shops (OMS) and Benedict Studios, resulting in very similar pieces. For example, the Craftsman Workshops' tall umbrella stand is found in several incarnations. Invariably, the ones bearing the Craftsman logo show better detailing, hammer marks, and richer patinas. While we do not like to overemphasize marks, this is one case where a company designation is likely to mean a difference in quality and value. An unmarked piece is probably the work of OMS or Benedict Studios.

Gustav Stickley's best metal pieces are architectural fireplace hoods; a series of pod plaques, of which the swirling pod is the best; a large pair of strapped candlesticks, about eighteen inches tall, all copper, with four flat, wrought straps ending in spades on the base; and an iron-and-copper coal scuttle. While some of Stickley's pairs of andirons are uninteresting, the best of them include a twenty-eight-inch-tall set with round balls at the top of each post, and his tapering-shaft andirons, measuring twenty-four inches tall. Finally, few makers made sets of fireplace tools, and Stickley's four-piece set (including the stand) is probably the best of the period.

Look for pieces with original patina, and ones free of post-manufacturing dents and flaws. It is important to note that many of these objects are die-stamped with the joiner's compass mark on their sides rather than underneath. Two marks are known, an earlier mark with the joiner's compass encircled by "The-Craftsman-Workshops-Gustav-Stickley" and a later mark of just the joiner's compass.

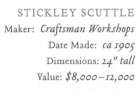

STICKLEY SCUTTLE
Maker: *Craftsman Workshops*
Date Made: *ca 1905*
Dimensions: *24" tall*
Value: *$8,000–12,000*

Gustav Stickley wrought iron and hammered copper coal scuttle with original dark brown patina.

Onondaga Metal Shops/Benedict Studios

Onondaga Metal Shops (OMS) was located in a small studio in downtown Syracuse at 581 South Clinton Street. In this diminutive shop, OMS produced fine hand-wrought copper and iron decorative accessories in the Arts and Crafts style. In 1907, Harry Benedict purchased OMS, and the company moved to the Benedict Manufacturing Company's plant in East Syracuse, after which their name was changed to Benedict Art Studios. *Fireside,* a monthly Syracuse business newsletter, stated in April 1942 that "OMS was operated independently of the main factory and under the name of Benedict Art Studios, producing fine hand wrought articles in copper, brass, and iron, which possessed unusual artistic qualities." OMS had become a part of Harry Benedict's expansion program. Arts and Crafts metal was, for the first time, being produced by the Benedict Manufacturing Company, continuing the designs of Onondaga Metal Shops.

We believe that OMS was actually doing work in the spirit of the period and that Benedict was a much more commercial concern. OMS preferred using only copper and iron, with the rare addition of brass, where Benedict often mixed brass with copper on individual pieces. Benedict boxes were produced in copper, with riveted brass corners. They also used brass handles on trays and for lids. We mention this because the two divisions often employed the same forms, and the OMS versions primarily relied on iron if a second metal was used. While pieces bearing the OMS mark are rare, those

BENEDICT STUDIO
COPPER CHARGER
Dimensions: *19" diameter*
Value: *$2,000–3,000*

Benedict Studios large wrought copper charger with stylized pods under a dark brown patina.

found are often closer in construction and spirit to objects made by Gustav Stickley's neighboring Craftsman Workshops.

OMS pieces show a finer, more subtle handling of the metal, where Benedict pieces often bear deliberate, deep hammer marks. Like Craftsman Workshops, OMS appears to have let the formation of the piece dictate the hammer marks. Ideally, the only hammer marks one should see on a piece of fine period copper are those needed to form the object.

Lesser makers such as Benedict often formed a piece in broad strokes and added the hammer marks to give the appearance of fine craftsmanship. For example, a Gustav Stickley nut bowl shows hammer marks that are lined up, traveling around the pieces and interlocking with alternating rows. It is clear that these were shaped by a hammer. It is worth noting, however, that all of the New York makers often started with spun forms, reserving the fine, finishing details for the hammer.

Both OMS and Benedict joined separate pieces of metal with rivets. Pieces with rivets were usually used on forms that did not originate with spun metal, such as umbrella stands and humidors. OMS's rivets were usually hand formed, while the uniformity of Benedict's rivets suggests they were initially cast.

Both firms used chemically induced patinas to achieve the warm brown effect of aged metal. OMS patinas have a more monochromatic, medium-brown color, while Benedict pieces usually started with a darker, black brown patina that was rubbed to show a piece's highlights.

The best pieces of OMS are, at times, similar to those of neighboring Craftsman Workshops. We have seen several extraordinary, early chargers with spade or pod decoration under rich, deep brown patinas. Other pieces include large round and rectangular trays, boxes, and candle sconces.

Jarvie

Robert Jarvie, originally from Schenectady, New York, moved to Chicago, Illinois. He worked for the city in various capacities until discovering that his first love was the Arts and Crafts movement. Jarvie experimented with book binding, cabinet making, and drawing before he began experimenting with interior lighting.

OMICRON CANDLESTICK

Maker: *Jarvie Omicron*

Dimensions: *11" tall*

Value: *$10,00–15,000*

Two-branch candlestick in turned brass with removable bobeches.

Jarvie's interest in early American and European designs was reflected in his earliest candle lanterns. Nevertheless, he did not begin to hit his stride as a designer until he put these personal reproductions aside and immersed himself in the more modern designs of the period.

While many American companies produced candlesticks, none measured up to the work of Robert Jarvie. He used the Greek alphabet to organize and name his designs, which have subsequently become some of the most sought-after objects produced during the period. The Iota stick, standing fourteen inches tall, or the Omicron, both in double and triple versions, would improve the finest of contemporary Arts and Crafts collections.

Known as the Candlestick Maker, Jarvie proved to be far more than that. He produced many commissions for trophies and awards, which are the best such examples made in America. He also designed and produced candle sconces with repoussé back plates, bookends, card trays, and simple hammered bowls. He was perhaps the only American designer who successfully used brass as the base metal for his pieces, though he also made objects out of copper, bronze, and silver.

Jarvie's brass patinas are exceptional, with a microcrystalline effect encrusted into their surface. It is also clear that some of his brass forms were left unpatinated, with the natural effects of oxidization forming a finish of its own over time. Look for large, heavy candlesticks, such as the Beta, Theta, or Kappa, with an undisturbed surface and larger repoussé pieces with a mellow milk-chocolate-colored patina.

Jarvie inspired a legion of imitators, though the quality and construction of his pieces was unparalleled. Jarvie sticks, for example, were cast and then lathe turned to accomplish the quality he was looking for. You can see, on their undersides, the spiraling marks of scored brass. Jarvie's best pieces usually bear at least his name, cut sharply into the metal like a hot knife into butter.

Dirk Van Erp

Dirk Van Erp is widely considered the most important metal-smith of the Arts and Crafts movement. There was a school of smithing in the San Francisco Bay area that included a number of fine artists, including Harry Dixon, August Tiesselinck, and William Van Erp, all of whom at one point worked under Dirk Van Erp's banner.

As with most American metalsmiths, Van Erp's early work remains the most important. It seems that these germinal efforts demanded the time and attention essential to defining his style. Later pieces often had most of these qualities but, due to the increased demand born of success, they lacked the power and spirit of those from his first period.

Van Erp learned his trade from his father in Holland, which accounts for his trademark windmill designation. He was initially employed by the Union Iron Works as a coppersmith, during which time he transformed shell casings left over from the Spanish American War into vases. He soon began selling these through gift shops and galleries in the San Francisco area.

Van Erp went into business for himself in 1908, with the firm remaining in family hands until 1977. He worked with the famous Chicago designer and craftsperson D'Arcy Gaw, who was thought to be responsible for the company's copper and mica table lamps. This partnership was established in March of 1910 and lasted for ten months.

VAN ERP JARDINIERE
Dimensions: 7" x 11"
Value: $7,000–8,000

Dirk Van Erp bulbous jardiniere with a warty surface under a dark brown patina. Early mark.

Dating Van Erp's pieces is fairly easy because of the marking system he used. All Van Erp pieces, when marked, bear both his windmill designation and the name Dirk Van Erp. The earliest mark has his name enclosed fully within a rectangular box. An important variation includes the name D'Arcy Gaw above his name. The next generation of pieces also includes Van Erp's name and the windmill, but the right-hand side of the box is tilted open. One explanation for this is that the original die-punch split from repeated use. Later pieces include the city, San Francisco.

Early pieces are heavy, have dark patinas, and show a great deal of handwork. Van Erp's consistent hammer marks are the

VAN ERP VASE
Dimensions: *4" tall*
Value: *$30,000–40,000*

Exceptional Dirk Van Erp squat vase with a rich red patina over a "curtained" body. Partial D'Arcy Gaw mark.

VAN ERP VASE

Dimensions: *10" tall*
Value: *$5,000–7,000*

Fine Dirk Van Erp bulbous vase with a broad shoulder and a rolled rim. Notice on the left the flashing of the dovetail joined metal, showing the piece was raised from flat copper.

work of a sure-handed master smithy. The rims of these early pieces are perfectly rolled, and the forms chosen were strong and robust. Pieces from this period were exclusively made of copper.

Open-Box period pieces were often lighter of scale and gauge, and the patinas tended to be lighter. The quality of handwork was also not as consistent, with some rims left unrolled and the hammering less sure. The one exception to these later works are red warty pieces, which remain among the most important of the period.

Red warty pieces are those where the deep, broad hammer marks imparted on the metal while raising sheet copper into hollowware forms were left in their raw state. Hence, the term *warty*. In addition, the red, rutile solution used during the forming process was left on the surface of the metal. Normally, Van Erp would add a brown patina to evenly cover the surface. As a result, red warty objects have a raw intensity to them that defines the process of their construction. This is not dissimilar to Gustav Stickley's use of quartered oak, the wild tiger-stripe grain serving as decoration that had been defined by the material and the process.

In addition, any red, warty piece is worthy of your consideration. These are rare and have remained the darlings of Arts and Crafts collectors. Also, look for larger vases of heavy gauge copper, with dark, rich patinas and fine hammered details.

Further Reading

I promised to provide a short reading list for those interested in more in-depth works on arts and crafts. I think it's best if I direct you towards specific authors rather than individual works. There are a number of writers who, over the years, penned some of the most important tomes on the Arts and Crafts. Here are my favorites:

DR. MARTIN EIDELBERG was one of the first important Arts and Crafts authors, and there is nothing he's written that isn't worthy of your library. His expertise goes far beyond the Arts and Crafts. But, for this field, it would be difficult to find a better place to start and finish.

DAVID CATHERS is another devoted and scholarly author whose love for the material is apparent in his work. I personally am interested in writing that isn't condescending—that is there to teach rather than impress. You should buy all he's written on the Arts and Crafts.

WENDY KAPLAN was the author of the catalog for the landmark exhibit The Art That Is Life, held at the Boston Museum of Fine Arts. She is currently the curator at the Los Angeles County Museum of Art. She is at once scholarly and accessible, and your library would not be complete without her contributions.

DR. EUGENE HECHT is a professor of physics and optics at Adelphi University in New York, and art pottery has been a serious hobby of his for nearly thirty years. While much of his writing has focused on the work of George Ohr, he writes with a great deal of love and passion about Arts and Crafts. You'll have fun reading his books, and you should have them.

GARTH CLARK is a contemporary ceramics dealer from Manhattan who has devoted his life to handling decorative ceramics and educating the masses about them. He is a gifted writer, and, while much of his writing focuses on material made after the Arts and Crafts period, you will learn much about decorative arts from him.

I HESITATE TO LIST MYSELF HERE not because I'm modest but because the writers mentioned above are simply better. I, however, have written several books on art pottery over the years that you may want to check out. The best of them is probably *Treasure or Not,* cowritten with my ageless bride Suzanne Perrault.

Index